Easy and Effective

Ways to
Communicate
with Parents

By Barbara Mariconda

SCHOLASTIC
PROFESSIONAL BOOKS

NEW YORK • TORONTO • LONDON • AUCKLAND • SYDNEY • MEXICO CITY
NEW DELHI • HONG KONG • BUENOS AIRES

To my mother,
Marion Johnson Morra, with love.

Cover design by **Josué Castilleja**
Interior design by **Holly Grundon**
Interior art by **Mike Moran**

ISBN: 0-439-29709-5
Copyright © 2003 by Barbara Mariconda
All rights reserved. Printed in the U.S.A.

5 6 7 8 9 10   40   09 08 07

Contents

Introduction

Some people seem to be born communicators; they always know what to say, and say it with grace and style. Their words make others comfortable in awkward situations, defuse tension, hit the nail on the head, and generally seem to bring out the best in those they're with. Call it charismatic, call it articulate, call it charming—whatever you call it, the truth is, these effective communicators possess a wide range of verbal skills that they use to best advantage. And contrary to what we may think, these communication skills are not always innate—they can be practiced and learned by just about anybody.

As teachers we're constantly involved in a variety of complex communication situations. We communicate with our students, with our colleagues, and with parents. Being able to use communication as a tool for building strong partnerships with parents is critical to the success of the students in our classrooms.

Communicating effectively with parents involves a number of techniques and skills that are highlighted throughout this book. The first chapter explores the nature and dynamics of the student-parent-teacher relationship. Chapter Two follows that up with concrete suggestions for starting the year off right and establishing positive contact early on. Selecting the best possible ways to communicate with parents and creating a range of strategies for communicating is outlined in Chapter Three, and Chapter Four presents techniques for defusing tension, should it arise. Every communication is made up of words, and Chapter Five looks at the power of words and the importance of listening well and choosing words carefully. Of course, at times, all educators must face the more difficult issues of neglect, abuse, or dealing with manipulative or overbearing parents. The final chapter examines and offers practical advice on how to deal with these challenges in a compassionate, professional way.

This book will explore, in depth, all of these aspects of parent-teacher communication. It will offer helpful tips for laying a strong groundwork, for preventing miscommunication, and for building rapport and mutual respect. From phone calls to conferences, open houses to e-mail, each is illustrated with actual examples, tips, and checklists, as well as many reproducible planning templates that will enhance your communication skills and make the juggling act that is teaching a whole lot less complicated.

Mastering the fine art of communication provides many benefits: It reduces anxiety and stress, increases confidence, and allows you to say what you mean and mean what you say in a constructive, proactive way.

But perhaps the greatest beneficiary of the rewards of a positive parent-teacher partnership is the child—because when parents and teachers work together for the best interest of the child, wonderful things can happen!

Chapter 1

The Parent-Teacher Partnership

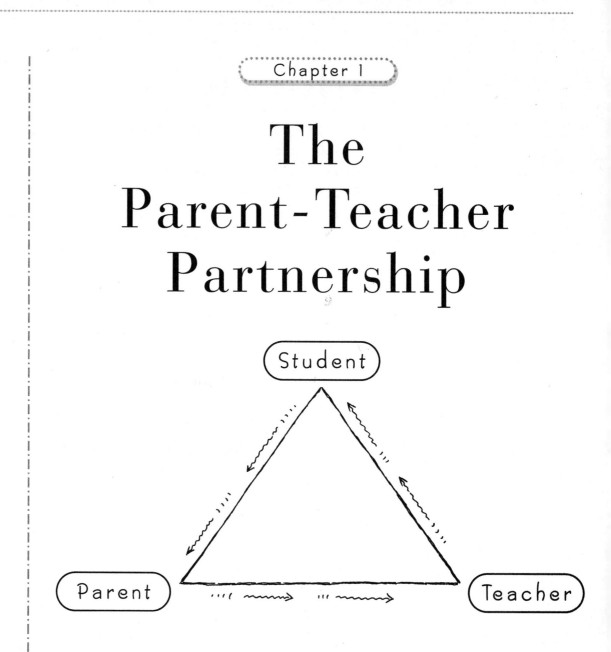

A s a parent of school-age children, each year I'd hold my breath through the first day of school, awaiting my son and daughter's return. I'd listen eagerly (and a little anxiously) taking in every word, every nuance, about that critical opening day. As a teacher, I wanted to get a sense of the academic challenge, level of creativity, management style, and discipline routines in each new classroom. But, more important, I always yearned to get the sense that my son and daughter would each be in a place with a caring adult, with someone who recognized, appreciated, and affirmed their unique (and sometimes quirky) gifts and attributes, and who would create an environment in which my precious children would be happy.

Being a parent as well as a teacher always put an interesting spin on my relationship with my kids' teachers. Sitting on the parent side of the conference table brought a deep level of empathy for the parents with whom I've conferred over the years. For, as a parent, the bottom line was this: my concern about any classroom matter was primarily in regard to one single, individual child—my own. While parents are aware that the teacher has about twenty other children to provide for, the fierce parental instinct puts the other nineteen in second place. This is a situation that every teacher and every parent has faced—a challenge that makes the teacher's job as educator, mediator, counselor, advocate, communicator, and confidante one of the most difficult, important jobs in the world.

Outside of the parents' influence, a teacher's influence can often affect a child more powerfully than any other adult relationship. For over 180 days, the child usually spends more waking hours with the classroom teacher than with any other individual adult. Parents and teachers shape, affect, inspire, and motivate children in both positive and negative ways. Because of this, the quality of the student-parent-teacher triangle is critical to the well-being, self-esteem, and social and academic growth of the child.

> Outside of the parents' influence, a teacher's influence can often affect a child more powerfully than any other adult relationship.

Throughout my years in the classroom, I've experienced the gamut of interpersonal exchanges with parents—delighted parents, thankful parents, curious parents, anxious, manipulative, involved, proud, excited, concerned, demanding, defensive, supportive, confused, and even hostile parents. As a parent I've also, if not walked in all of those parental shoes, certainly tried them all on for size. And what I've learned is that when parents understand and believe that the teacher always acts in the best interest of the child, an attitude of trust and mutual respect will emerge. Trust and mutual respect are the blocks that build a unified parent-teacher team that can truly affect children in powerful, meaningful, and long-lasting ways.

Ultimately, building a parent-teacher relationship on mutual respect and trust is just as important as the ability to teach reading or math. In fact, it will not only prevent burn-out, it will nurture long-lasting, respectful relationships with parents and students that can last a lifetime.

Keeping the Right Focus:
A Parent-Teacher Mission Statement

I sometimes wish there were a credo or a broad, universal mission statement for parents and teachers—an umbrella statement that would shape every parent-teacher-student interaction. In my mind, that mission statement would read something like this:

> Our shared top priority as parents and teachers is to consider the best interest of the child.

If all parties accepted the mission statement, and trusted that all decisions in regard to the child were based on this belief, wouldn't there be fewer misunderstandings, fewer resentments and less blaming that, in the end, only hurt the student? Wouldn't teachers be more understanding of parents, parents more supportive of teachers, and wouldn't students ultimately benefit by having a unified team of adults on their side?

The Educational Triangle:
Student-Parent-Teacher

If only it were as simple as writing the mission statement on a piece of poster board and hanging it in the classroom! In fact, few parents or teachers would disagree with this mission statement. Yet, until a deep level of trust is built among the points of what I call the educational triangle—student, parent, and teacher—it is difficult to put our mission statement into practice.

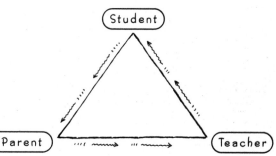

This framework is the ideal support system for students. The foundation on which a successful educational program is built is a strong partnership between parents and teacher. This partnership lifts up the student, who benefits from the consistency of adult support and assistance, both at home and at school.

However, in the real world of the classroom, we are never just dealing with the situation at hand, but with the unique personalities, past life experiences, expectations, prejudices, and sensitivities both conscious and unconscious, that make us all tick. It is easy to see how this undercurrent of personality and life experience can enhance or undermine each parent-teacher exchange.

Stepping Out of the Box: The Parent Perspective

Let's take a look at the parent-teacher dynamic underlying three different communication scenarios (pages 10–12). In each scenario, the parent is upset, the teacher is stressed, and the student continues to behave in negative ways. No one is happy. In fact, resentment is building up among all parties. The teacher looks to the parent for support, the parent looks to the teacher for a solution, and the student looks to any adult at all to take charge.

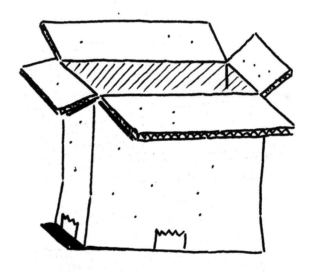

What isn't clear in each exchange is the fact that each player—the student, the teacher, and the parent—reacts not only to the situation at hand, but is shaped and motivated by past experience, insecurities, fears, and expectations often unknown to the others involved. Now, let's look at a series of "what-ifs" that could affect the parent-teacher partnership.

Scenario 1

Ms. Cooper telephones Mark Avery's mother because he has been acting out and fooling around in class. He has not been able to complete independent class work. Mrs. Avery states that her son is bored and is not challenged enough in the classroom, which is why he is acting out. She implies that if Ms. Cooper were more interesting, or if her lessons were more stimulating, the problem would be solved. Ms. Cooper suggests that Mark is not bored, and asks Mrs. Avery to follow through at home. Mrs. Avery feels that this is a school problem, and that the teacher ought to handle it in school. Ms. Cooper believes that the parent is copping out and begins to feel defensive about her teaching. She secretly worries that perhaps she *is* boring. The tension across the telephone line is almost audible. Ms. Cooper will try to jazz up her lessons a little, and will avoid calling Mark's mother in the future.

A case
of shifting
blame

Scenario 1

(REVISITED)

What if...

Mark's mother, Mrs. Avery, cannot control Mark at home and is at the end of her rope. Her husband and mother have both criticized her parenting, and place the blame for Mark's behavior squarely on her shoulders. Mrs. Avery is upset, feeling overwhelmed and guilty. Ms. Cooper's call put her right over the top. She isn't about to share her perceived inadequacies with Ms. Cooper—does she really need another adult viewing her as incompetent? And what if Ms. Cooper is new to her school and working for an extremely critical administrator. Mrs. Avery's comments play directly into her insecurity in her new position.

Suggestion

For tips on ways to phrase behavioral concerns to avoid negative connotations, see page 63.

Rachel has been having difficulty on the playground. She is manipulative with the other girls, trying to pit one against the other, and each day someone comes inside in tears. Mr. Sanders has witnessed this behavior, and has spoken to Rachel about the value of playing together rather than excluding others. Rachel blames the others and after several weeks of this, finds herself the child left out. Rachel's mom, Mrs. Sheridan calls Mr. Sanders and demands that he call the parents of the other girls, and that he discipline them for excluding Rachel. When he tries to explain what's been happening, Mrs. Sheridan accuses him of taking sides and threatens that she will take the matter up with the principal.

Excluded child—angry parent

Scenario 2
(REVISITED)

What if...

Mrs. Sheridan, Rachel's mother, is heartbroken to see her second-grade daughter as an "outcast." She remembers her years on the outside of the popular crowd, and vows that her daughter will not suffer in the same way. She will continue to insist that Mr. Sanders intervene. How else will Rachel ever be included? On the other hand, what if Mr. Sanders, the youngest of six brothers, cannot stand feeling "bossed around"? Mrs. Sheridan and Rachel are both pushing the button that triggers resistance in him, and he will fall into an unconscious yet familiar passive-aggressive role. He will do little and hope the situation takes care of itself.

Suggestion

For ways to effectively respond to an angry parent, see page 64.

Jack comes off the school bus each morning with a pink slip in his hand. The bus driver has written him up again, for any number of transgressions aboard the bus. He yells, teases other students, refuses to sit in his seat, punches another boy, and chews gum. After the second warning in a week's time, his teacher, Mrs. Ramos, calls Jack's mother, Ms. Gunther to inform her that once again Jack has lost his bus-riding privileges and that she will need to transport him to school. Ms. Gunther sighs, says (in an exhausted tone) that "he'll get it when he comes home," and apologizes for the hundredth time. From experience Mrs. Ramos knows that Jack will not "get it" when he gets home, and that Ms. Gunther is too worn out to follow through with anything besides a minute or two of yelling. Jack will enjoy a car ride with his overburdened mother for another day or two before he winds up back on the bus again.

Privilege or punishment?

Scenario 3
(REVISITED)

What if...

Mrs. Ramos knows enough about Ms. Gunther to know that she works two jobs, is constantly exhausted, but that she tries her best. But what if Ms. Gunther's ex-husband continually tells Jack that his mother works too much and that maybe Jack should come to live with him, out of state, that after all, it would be easier for his mother. What if Ms. Gunther secretly wonders if her ex-husband isn't right, and then feels terribly guilty. So, if a car ride into school will provide a few extra minutes together, why not? And what if Mrs. Ramos, herself a single super-mom, prides herself on being consistent, strong, and present to her own children, managing a job and parenting with apparent ease? Would it be easy for her to relate to Ms. Gunther?

Suggestion

For tips on setting communication ground rules and selecting ways of communicationg with parents that work for you, see Chapter 3.

Selecting the Best Possible Ways to
Communicate With Parents

Vehicles of Communication That Work for You

This sampling of fictional what-ifs make up the complex undercurrent that can drag parent-teacher relationships down. I'm not suggesting that teachers analyze parents' every word to root out their "what-ifs," just as teachers would not appreciate parents similarly analyzing them.

What I am suggesting is that we recognize that parents and teachers alike respond not only to the obvious, but to a wide array of outer and inner influences. This recognition helps defuse anger and blame, and will enable you to respond objectively to things that may have as much to do with a "what-if" as with the situation at hand. With this in mind, you can guide parent-teacher relationships in more productive ways, redirecting the conversation back to the common goal of the welfare and best interest of the child.

Putting It into Practice

The mission statement, to first consider the best interest of the child, is the mortar that holds the parent-teacher-student triangle together, the boat that floats each classroom policy. Keeping the mission statement in mind, every communication you have with parents should:

◎ be undertaken with the ultimate goal of helping the student.

◎ provide information.

◎ take place in the context of established, familiar, consistent, well-defined classroom expectations and rules.

◎ be sensitive to individual circumstances.

◎ be carried out in an objective, compassionate, and professional manner.

In following these points, a teacher communicates a clear, reassuring message that:

◎ defuses tension through communication.

◎ calms anxiety with objectivity and concern.

◎ dispels confusion with information.

◎ transforms manipulation into teamwork.

◎ neutralizes hostility with understanding and empathy.

The rest of this book examines how to practically apply this mission statement to the day-to-day challenges of classroom life. The focus is on communication and the multitude of opportunities for establishing trust and a sense of mutual purpose.

Chapter 2

Starting the Year Off Right!

(Or, Prevention Is the Best Medicine!)

Ask parents when the school year really begins, and they'll agree that it is long before the first day of school! In fact, the minute the class list is announced at the end of the previous school year, teachers, parents, and students alike begin to think about the year ahead. This is the prime time for starting the next year off right and establishing positive lines of communication.

Before the First Bell Rings:
A Communication Toolbox

There are a number of simple yet effective tools I've used for team building with parents and students before and during the first days of the new school year. During the summer months, though the beach may beckon, it's worth spending a little time planning for and using several of these key communication tools. These include a student welcome card, a parent welcome letter, the "Getting to Know Your Child" Questionnaire, a parent and student welcome back orientation, and the back-to-school phone call. All of this actually takes less effort than you might think, and the positive impression parents come away with is a terrific return on your investment of time and energy! . . . And after you've used each of these tools just once, you've created a basic prototype that you can reuse year after successful year.

The Student Welcome Card

Somewhere between the end of one school year and the beginning of the next, a welcome letter is in order—and the sooner, the better! I always send an upbeat, colorful welcome card to students with a short personalized message. My objective is to make each child feel comfortable and welcome. I often wait until I leave for vacation and purchase post cards for this purpose. As soon as I receive my class list, I make a database with names and addresses so that I can easily print address labels. I send a separate welcome letter to parents that includes a "Getting to Know Your Child" questionnaire that they can fill out and return to me. In this way I get a clear sense of the parents' perspective on their child's strengths and areas of concern. This welcome letter is my opportunity, before the first bell rings, to share the credo, build trust, and reach out in a positive way to parents and children. Some sample post cards and letters follow.

TIPS

5 Tips
for Writing Exciting
Welcome Back Postcards

❋ Include a personalized greeting.

❋ Tell the student something interesting about yourself.

❋ Express your excitement about the coming year.

❋ Invite the student to the Welcome Back Orientation.

❋ Include wishes for a fun-filled and safe summer.

Hello Danny!
Greetings from your new second-grade teacher. I am so eager to meet you. There are many fun, exciting, and interesting things to learn and do in second grade! I know we will enjoy a terrific year together. Hope to see you at our Welcome Back Orientation from 10:00-11:00 A.M. on August 28th! In the meantime, have a fun-filled and safe summer!

Love,
Mrs. "M"

I try to make each letter personal rather than copying the same letter over and over. Here's another variation:

Hi Rachel!
Did you realize that your new second-grade teacher is visiting the Grand Canyon and thinking about you? It's true! While I'm enjoying this vacation, I can't help but look forward to meeting you. There are many fun, exciting, and interesting things to learn and do in grade 2. I can hardly wait to begin our year together. Hope to see you at our Welcome Back Orientation from 10:00-11:00 A.M. on August 28th! Until then, have a fun-filled and safe summer!

Love,
Mrs. "M"

The Parent Welcome Letter and "Getting to Know Your Child" Questionnaire

Here is a sample of the parent welcome letter and accompanying "Getting to Know Your Child" Questionnaire: (I create this parent letter and reproduce it, sending a personally signed copy to each household.)

Dear Parents,

I'd like to take this opportunity to introduce myself to you. As a Grade 2 teacher at _____ School, I will have the pleasure of spending the next school year with your son or daughter! I am excited about the year ahead, and am looking forward to meeting you and your child.

During the coming year, your child and I will be spending many, many hours in the classroom together. And I want you to know that there is no place I would rather be, and no job that I would rather have. Together, as parents and teacher, we can truly provide a comfortable, stimulating, nurturing, and challenging environment for your child. My promise to you is that I will consistently put the best interest of your child first, keep you informed about your child's growth and classroom activities, and always welcome your input and support. As the year progresses, I also encourage you to contact me with any concerns, questions, or comments you might have. You can always leave a message for me at the school office, write me a note, or e-mail me at _____ .

Second grade is a stimulating, exciting place to be! We'll focus on developing a wide range of reading skills and strategies through the use of quality literature and phonics. As a second grader, your child will be provided with many creative writing experiences, and a wide range of hands-on math activities that will encourage critical thinking. Social studies and science units on everything from the Pilgrims, communities, and the rain forest, to insects, electricity, and map skills will also motivate young learners. Much of our curriculum is integrated, which means that themes we are exploring in reading are often related to a unit in social studies or science, word problems in math mirror vocabulary presented in reading and spelling. I also work hard to structure lessons to meet the needs of all learning styles, so that each of my students will have a wide range of vehicles for learning.

Enclosed is a simple "Getting to Know Your Child" Questionnaire. This questionnaire will help provide some basic information you'd like me to know about your child. Your responses help me get to know your child more quickly and raise my awareness of your child's likes and dislikes, interests, strengths, and challenges. Please fill it out and return it to me as soon as possible. My address follows:

Barbara Mariconda

_____ Elementary School

_____ Street

City, State, zip

Also, please bring your child along to my Welcome Back Orientation on August 28th, from 10:00-11:00 A.M., in our classroom, room 16. This is an opportunity for us to meet, and for you and your child to take a tour of the classroom, and be introduced to the wonderful world of Grade 2! Refreshments will be served.

Have a wonderful summer! Hope to see you on August 28th.

Sincerely,

Barbara Mariconda

Getting to Know Your Child

Questionnaire

Dear Parent,
Please fill out the following questionnaire and return it to me at:

_____

1. Child's name _____   Birthday _____

2. I'd describe my son/daughter as _____

   _____

3. One important thing for you to know about my son/daughter is

   _____

4. What does your child like best about school?

   _____

5. Her/his strengths include

   _____

   _____

6. List some of the activities your child is most interested or involved in.

   _____

7. What hopes or goals do you have for your child in second grade?

   _____

Feel free to use the back of this page for any additional comments or information you'd like to share. Thank you!

Signed _____
          PARENT'S NAME

Parent and Student Welcome Back Orientation

In my district teachers are given one or two "prep days" prior to the opening of school for the purpose of setting up their classrooms. Since these prep days are usually not long enough to really get the job done, teachers regularly stay into the evening to complete the name tags, bus lists, and bulletin boards in time for the first day of school. And, in the midst of all of this work it is common practice for parents to stroll in with their son or daughter, requesting a tour of the classroom, engaging the teacher in conversation, and many times looking for a mini-conference about their child. You may have had a similar experience and found yourself torn between the task of finishing your preparation work and taking time to establish a rapport with a parent. However, if you have a class of twenty-five students and the parents of half of them drop in for a visit, much of your precious prep time is simply lost.

While it's beneficial for everyone to meet prior to the first day of school, it's easy to see how teachers may appear preoccupied, rushed, or less than fully engaged during these impromptu visits. For this reason, I usually designate one hour during my pre-September prep days as a parent and student Welcome Back Orientation. I select a time for parents and students to stop by for an informal tour in which I give a very brief overview of our classroom schedule, review special activities and policies, and invite everyone to share in some refreshments. (Be sure to clear this with your administrator, as having visitors may create security issues.) The objective of the orientation is to make students and their parents feel welcome, to generate excitement about the coming year, and to explain to parents what the lines of communication will be. The date and time of this orientation is included in my welcome letter. The agenda items on my Welcome Back Orientation to-do list, including what to plan, share, and discuss, appear in the Tips box, at right.

I always tried to piggyback this orientation onto another meeting or school commitment, as a polite means of drawing it to a close on time. The temptation to stay on and chat

To-Do List

* ❋ Write a daily schedule on the board.

* ❋ Make seating arrangements. (Let students find their desks and try them out.)

* ❋ Conduct a classroom "tour" that highlights special areas of the room, such as the reading corner, class library, bulletin boards, fish tank, and so forth.

* ❋ Mention classroom "highlights" to look forward to: dissecting owl pellets, learning stations, the winter holiday play, specific field trips, and such.

* ❋ List necessary school supplies for the first day of school.

* ❋ Offer simple, non-messy refreshments such as juice, cookies, and pretzels.

informally may be great, but in this way you can easily lose another valuable hour of prep time. When the orientation hour is nearing its end, glance at your watch and announce, "Our time is almost up, and I have a grade level meeting in about 2 minutes. I'm so glad you were all able to come, and I'll see you all on the first day of school!" If you have any papers or notices for parents or students, you can distribute them at the door as they leave. Then, head right off to your meeting. Avoid staying in the classroom at the close of the orientation, as it may seem like an invitation for eager parents and students to stay on (and on and on . . .).

The Back-to-School Phone Call

We've all made it through the first week or so of school. New friendships are being forged, old friendships renewed, new routines established, and all of us are, for the most part, still on our best behavior. This is the time when there are a million things to do, but tops on my list is the back-to-school phone call.

I make it a point to call every household on my class list within the first two weeks of the school year with something positive to say about each child. It's interesting to note that parents are often initially suspicious or slightly defensive as soon as I say hello. They'll even sometimes respond to my "Hi, it's Ellen's teacher, Mrs. Mariconda. How are you?" with an anxious, "Yes, well, what's the problem?"

I love to hear the change in parents' tone of voice as I explain that I was calling to say how much I'm enjoying getting to know their son or daughter, and to let them know how well he or she is doing. I make certain to note something positive about even those students who are having some difficulty in the transition to a new grade level. I share a particular incident or observation that illustrates my point. I do not minimize any difficulty they might be experiencing but simply point out something positive about their efforts, determination, spirit, or personality. I use this opportunity to ask parents how they perceive their child's adjustment to the new year and to stress again that I will be in close touch with them throughout the school year. The key is to be positive.

There will always be students with learning, behavioral, or social issues, of which parents are usually well aware. These parents are often used to hearing from the teacher only when he or she is at wit's end or has a serious concern. It's especially important to reassure these parents (but not to mislead them into thinking that their child's issues have mysteriously disappeared) that first and foremost you enjoy having their child in class and intend to be on their side throughout the school year.

HOW TO ESTABLISH THE RIGHT TONE: THE FIRST PHONE CALL

The following conversations adapted from several back-to-school phone calls highlight positive ways to approach an introductory call.

The First Call:
Sample One

Mrs. M: Good evening, Mrs. Hastings?

Mrs. Hastings: Yes?

Mrs. M: It's Barbara Mariconda, Katie's teacher, how are you?

Mrs. Hastings: I'm fine. What's up? (A little anxiety creeps into her voice.)

Mrs. M: I'm just calling to tell you what a smooth transition Katie's made into second grade!

Mrs. Hastings: Really! How nice! (Evident relief.) She does seem to enjoy going to school.

Mrs. M: I'm delighted to hear that! She is a pleasure to have in class—very attentive, and a hard worker. I also admire the kind way she treats her classmates. She is really a friend to all and a great role model for her peers. As a matter of fact, the other day Katie approached a new student of ours who had no one to play with and invited her to play on the tire swing. (The specific example shows the parent that you are involved and aware and that her child is perceived as special.)

Mrs. Hastings: Yes, Katie is a nice kid! (You can almost hear the smile and the pride in her voice.) How is she doing with her reading? She really struggled last year. (The anxiety creeps back in.)

Mrs. M: I'll be monitoring everyone's reading very closely over the coming weeks and I've already been paying close attention to identify each child's strengths and weaknesses. My plan is to build up Katie's sight vocabulary so that she'll have a broader base of words that are familiar. As we move along, I'll probably send home a list of basic sight words for Katie to practice.

Mrs. Hastings: I'm so glad you're on top of this. (She is relieved and feels that Katie is in competent, caring hands.) What can we do to help?

Mrs. M: Well, I'm always pleased to have parents' input and support! (Affirming the importance of the parent's role.) When I send home the word lists you might want to make up some flash cards for review. I'd be happy to meet with you to show you how to do this and how to work with her at home. I'm thinking of inviting a number of parents in so we can all work together. Of course, reading together is a big plus.

Mrs. Hastings: My husband and I will be happy to do that.

Mrs. M: Terrific! We'll talk again soon!

Mrs. Hastings: Thanks—it was great hearing from you. (It is apparent that she really means it!)

Mrs. M: I enjoyed it as well! Remember, I'm always here to answer any questions you might have. You can call me at the office, e-mail me, or send a note. I'm always happy to discuss Katie's progress. (Remind the parent that you are always available to listen to his or her concerns.)

Mrs. Hastings: Thanks so much!

Sample Two

Mrs. M: Good evening, Mr. Labelle?

Mr. Labelle: Yes?

Mrs. M: It's Barbara Mariconda, Danny's teacher. How are you?

Mr. Labelle: Good. (Silence—he's waiting for a negative behavior report.)

Mrs. M: I'm just touching base to let you know how well Danny is adjusting to sixth grade!

Mr. Labelle: Really?

Mrs. M: Absolutely. He has a really engaging personality—so full of energy and enthusiasm! (A positive way to describe the overly active child.) He's extremely popular with his peers as well.

Mr. Labelle: He's energetic all right! I'm surprised he isn't driving you crazy, especially with all this changing classes you do. (The parent is expressing concerns about behavior.)

Mrs. M:	No, not at all. In fact, I'm used to twelve-year-old boys with extra energy—it comes with the territory! (Eases the parent's concern.) Besides, Danny and I already have an understanding about the importance of moving quietly between classes. This is the first time that students have changed classes for reading and math. I've explained how important it is ˈ t to disturb others during these transitions. After a reminder or two, Danny seems to be making a real effort to move quickly and quietly, and I expect he'll continue to develop even stronger self-control as the year goes on. (Describes the challenge, affirms Danny's efforts, indicates that the teacher is on top of the situation.)
Mr. Labelle:	Good. Glad to hear it.
Mrs. M:	Remember, I'm always here to answer any questions you might have. You can call me at the office, e-mail me, or send a note. I'm always happy to discuss Danny's progress. (Remind the parents that you are eager to listen to their concerns.)
Mr. Labelle:	Thanks so much!

Phone Tips

Keys to a Successful Back-to-School Phone Call

✳ Call as early in the school year as possible.

✳ The first phone call to parents should ALWAYS be positive.

✳ Highlight a strength the child has.

✳ Be specific in your praise of the child. Avoid words like *nice* and *good*. Instead, give a specific example or an anecdote to illustrate your point.

✳ Address obvious areas of concern by:

    1. Acknowledging the challenge.

    2. Describing a positive way that you've addressed the challenge.

    3. Expressing confidence that you and the student will continue to work successfully together on a particular issue.

    4. Assuring the parent that you welcome their insights and feedback.

✳ Remind parents that they can contact you with any concerns and encourage them to do so through established lines of communication. Be sure to include specific hours when you can accept phone calls. (For more tips on setting communication ground rules, see Chapter 3.)

Back-to School

Communication Quick Tips and Checklist

☐ Send students each a personalized welcome card prior to the start of school in order to make them feel welcome and to generate some excitement about the year ahead.

☐ Send each parent a welcome letter to set a positive tone, and to discuss and highlight special activities.

☐ Include a "Getting to Know Your Child Questionnaire" for parents to fill out and return to you which will reveal parental concerns or other pertinent information about their child.

☐ Plan a Welcome Back Orientation in order to meet parents and students on your terms, and introduce them to your classroom in a way that reduces anxiety and is casual, yet informative.

☐ Get things off to a great start by making a positive back-to-school phone call to each household.

Keeping It Organized: The Parent Contact Log

Use the following back to school contact log to keep track of when and how you've made contact with each family. The log becomes increasingly useful when you jot down parents' full names, how they wish to be addressed, and any pertinent notes about the communication you've had in the last column.

Continue the communication log through the rest of the year by copying and triple hole-punching the contact log and placing these copies in a binder, behind the initial contact sheets you've completed. Use this binder to collect

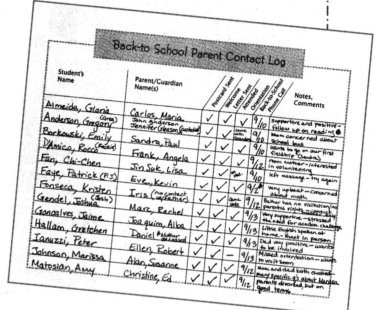

any ongoing communications, notes, and correspondences. You may want to add to the back of the binder a class set of tabbed dividers (dividers with pockets are especially handy). Write each student's name on a tab and use this section to sort and organize any signed forms or correspondences you need to keep permanently such as the Parent Conference Call Planner on pages 67 and 68, and the "Getting to Know You" Questionnaire on page 18. This makes a great quick reference file for conferences.

Establishing these quick tips as a part of your back-to-school routine will go a long way toward laying a strong foundation on which positive, trusting parent-teacher relationships can be built!

Back-to School Parent Contact Log

Student's Name	Parent/Guardian Name(s)	Postcard Sent	Welcome Letter Sent	Orientation Attended	Back-to-School Phone Call	Notes & Comments

Chapter 3

Selecting the Best Possible Ways to

Communicate With Parents

Perhaps the best way to avoid misunderstandings with parents is to have regular, clear, established lines of communication with them. The more they know, and the more they are included in the goings-on of the classroom, the more they'll feel a part of the team. Informed parents who feel included on a regular basis are more likely to be supportive and understanding, and less likely to jump to negative conclusions.

Vehicles of Communication That Work for You

You've already set a positive tone with your welcome letters, questionnaire, and orientation. You've impressed parents with your level of commitment through the back-to-school phone call. Continue to build on this positive foundation by establishing your communication vehicles before any questions arise. Here is a list of communication tools that get rave reviews from parents:

◎ Weekly or biweekly newsletter

◎ E-mail version of newsletter

◎ Classroom Web site

◎ Autumn Open House

◎ Telephone conferences

◎ Regular office hours for parent conferences

◎ Classroom volunteering

In this chapter, we'll look at each of these communication vehicles and highlight the mutual benefits for parents, students, and teachers. Quick tips on how to create and establish these procedures in ways that are practical and realistic will also be provided. But, before we jump aboard, there are several "ground rules" which drive each vehicle and help keep all of your communications on track and effective.

Communication Ground Rules

1. **Always tell parents immediately how and when you'll communicate with them.** Let them know that you value their questions and concerns and would never minimize them by responding "off the cuff" or "on the fly." Explain that in order to give them your undivided attention, you've set aside specific times to talk. It's important to decide when you want to take and return phone calls and e-mails, when you're available for after or before school conferences (I've always preferred the before school conference because of the built-in time parameters), and to actually be available during those times. If your school policy requires that you remain in the building for 30 minutes beyond the regular school day, you might want to designate certain days for phone conferences and others for in-school conferences. Then, post these times and procedures and send them home with your welcome letter or first newsletter. Earmarking office hours and sticking to them eliminates the need parents may feel to grab your ear in the parking lot, or monopolize your attention outside your classroom door before or after school.

2. **Never feel pressured to make an important decision, evaluation, or assessment during a parent conference or conversation.** Instead, be prepared to take some time to think and get back to the parent. For example, "You've made a great point, Mrs. Smith, and this is an important issue. I'd really like to give it some serious thought and get back to you on it." Then, make it a point to tell the parent exactly when they can expect a response: "Let's schedule another meeting/phone conference for Friday. Does that work for you?" This allows you time to consider the issue, develop possible solutions, and consult with colleagues, administrators, or other professionals, if necessary.

3. **Establish yourself as someone parents can trust.** Be discrete: Avoid discussing students with other parents or engaging in any negative faculty-room talk that sometimes takes place. I also make this a rule for parent volunteers who spend time in the classroom. I tell parents that all of us have had good days and bad days. If a volunteer witnesses a "bad day"—any negative or challenging behavior on the part of a student in the class—that particular situation remains confidentially in the classroom. (For more on parent volunteers, see page 46.)

4. **Assure parents that you will inform them immediately about any concerns you might have with regard to their child.** Parents become extremely upset when the first sign of trouble comes in the form of a progress report halfway into the marking period, or worse yet, on the report card itself. I always try to share even small concerns early on, rather than waiting and then dropping a bombshell.

5. **When presenting a concern to parents, ALWAYS be ready to explain what strategies you've already used to address the issue, and what new strategies you are considering.** Parents don't want concerns dropped in their laps without at least a tentative action plan, which you'll adjust based on their input. (It would be a little like a doctor calling with less than perfect test results, but with no idea how to treat the symptoms!)

If you keep these communication ground rules in mind, parents will thank you, and your life as a classroom teacher will be much easier!

Now, let's look at the key components of a successful communication system that will keep parents informed and on your side.

Weekly or Biweekly Newsletter

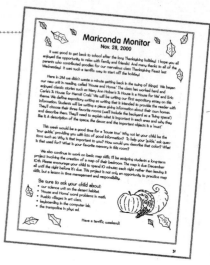

How many times have you heard parents describe the following parent-child exchange?

> Parent: Hi honey, how was school?
>
> Child: Good.
>
> Parent: So, what did you do today?
>
> Child: Oh, nothing.

A simple weekly newsletter is a terrific way to keep parents informed about curriculum, class activities, and special events. It also serves as an all-important jumping off point for parent-child conversation about school. Here are some pointers to help you create a successful newsletter—one that will not only provide information, but will stimulate conversation between parents and children. The newsletter should always

- ◎ focus on the positive.
- ◎ describe key units, themes, or topics.
- ◎ reinforce/review classroom policies, new goals and objectives.
- ◎ praise student effort.
- ◎ include an "Ask your child about:" section.
- ◎ outline field trip and special events dates and deadlines.
- ◎ express gratitude for parental support.

Take a look at the sample newsletter on the following page. Evaluate it from two objectives—those of teacher and parent:

1. The teacher's objective is to keep parents informed, generate parental support (both academic and emotional), and review and reinforce class policies.

2. The parents' objective is to understand what is going on in the classroom. The newsletter serves as a barometer against which they can gauge their child's progress. In sum, the newsletter should inform, set expectations, and be sensitive to parents' concerns.

A successful newsletter—whether it is simple and straight forward or very detailed—will address both objectives.

Mariconda Monitor
Nov. 28, 2000

It was good to get back to school after the long Thanksgiving holiday! I hope you all enjoyed the opportunity to relax with family and friends! And many thanks to all of the parents who contributed goodies for our marvelous class Thanksgiving Feast last Wednesday! It was such a terrific way to start off the holiday!

Here in 2M we didn't waste a minute getting back in the swing of things! We began our new unit in reading, called "House and Home." The class has worked hard and enjoyed classic stories such as Mary Ann Hoban's "A House Is a House for Me" and Eric Carle's "A House for Hermit Crab." We will be writing our first expository essay on this theme. We define expository writing as writing that is intended to provide the reader with information. Students will be writing a piece giving information about their own homes. They'll choose their three favorite rooms (we'll include the backyard as a "living space") and describe them. They'll need to explain what is important in each area and why they like it. A description of the space, the decor, and the important objects is a "must."

This week would be a good time for a "house tour." Why not let your child be the "tour guide," providing you with lots of good information? To help your "guide," ask questions such as: Why is that important to you? How would you describe that color? What is that used for? What is your favorite memory in this room?

We also continue to work on basic map skills. I'll be assigning students a long-term project involving the creation of a map of their bedroom. The map is due December 10th. Please encourage your child to spend 10 minutes each night, rather than leaving it all until the night before it's due. This project is not only an opportunity to practice map skills, but a lesson in time management and responsibility.

Be sure to ask your child about:
- our science unit on the desert habitat,
- "House and Home" word problems in math,
- Pueblo villages in art class,
- keyboarding in the computer lab,
- the trampoline in phys ed.

Have a terrific weekend!

Here's another sample newsletter format. This teacher has her sixth-grade class write short "columns" on a variety of topics and ends with her own note to parents.

What's New in 6-N

Reading

We in 6-N love to read! We're studying author Katherine Paterson and reading her wonderful book The Great Gilly Hopkins. We're comparing it to her other Newbery Award winning book Bridge to Terabithia. You might even want to read these books. We think that even parents would love these terrific stories.

Museum Trip

Our trip to the Phelps Museum was very exciting. We saw their Egyptian exhibit. This helped us with our Egyptian research papers, which are due next week. We've been busy making Egyptian art projects. Some of us did paper mâché mummy masks, others did hieroglyphics scrolls. We have learned a lot about ancient Egyptian Civilization.

Math

Can you multiply fractions? We in 6 - N have become experts at this. Are you up to a challenge? Try these examples and have your kid correct them.

$1/3 \times 2/5 = ?$
$3/4 \times 5/8 = ?$
$7/13 \times 1/8 = ?$

Answers will appear in next week's newsletter!

Congratulations to the Following Students:

Jason Parker won our class math triathlon, with Jenny Ponatowski coming in a close second. Maria Nieves made the Principal's Board for good citizenship and received a blue ribbon. Did you know that the following students got perfect spelling tests three weeks in a row? Kate Thompson, Lawanda Porter, and Roberto Fernez are the class spelling aces! And, the class salutes Kevin O'Connor for reading to our first graders.

Notes from Mrs. Nunez

I'm so pleased with the progress the class is making! The students are doing a super job with their research papers on ancient Egypt, they're mastering simple sentence diagramming, and are engaging in many important conversations about *The Great Gilly Hopkins*.

Be sure to ask about: Our Unit Spelling Test next week, Computer Lab Project on databases, and our three-part harmony in chorus! I also hope you've noticed the super job our class reporters have been doing in putting this newsletter together! Bravo 6-N!

Newsletter Planning Tips

In planning your newsletter, you might find the following planner helpful.

Date: _____

Important Units: _____

Reading/Writing: _____

Math: _____

Social Studies: _____

Science: _____

Other: _____

Field Trips: _____

Projects/Homework: _____

A Particularly Praiseworthy Effort: _____

Dates to Remember: _____

Need a few handy lead-in lines for your newsletter? Try these:

Have you heard about . . . ?

Another exciting project is . . .

The class is enjoying . . .

We're working really hard on . . .

Were you aware that . . . ?

We know you'll enjoy hearing about . . .

Another terrific project is . . .

Don't forget about . . .

Be sure to check out . . .

The class is abuzz about . . .

The E-Mail Newsletter

A modern-day variation on the newsletter is to paste the document copy into an e-mail or send the letter as an attachment to parents who are regularly on-line. In the beginning of the school year, you can ask parents for their e-mail addresses, create a parent contact list, and "batch" send the newsletter. Parents can e-mail you back with questions or comments. Paula Healey, a veteran first-grade teacher from Fairfield, Connecticut, regularly uses this e-mail option. She was initially concerned about receiving too many e-mails from parents, and worried that she wouldn't have the time to answer them. What actually happened was that the e-mail option eliminated numerous phone calls and the frustration of time-consuming phone tag that is the by-product of the answering machine/voice-mail era.

Whether via good old-fashioned paper or e-mail, the newsletter should be sent home once every two weeks, at a minimum. I always aimed for a newsletter every Friday, but realistically, some weeks were just too busy. However, once you have a format established, creating the newsletter becomes easy. Boldface the key points, indent new topics, and keep a file from year to year. Since curriculum often stays relatively consistent over time, you can simply modify last year's newsletters to reflect basic curriculum information and then replace dates, specific feedback, and current events; the basic format will remain the same.

TIPS

Newsletter

❋ Be sure to always spell-check and have a colleague proofread your newsletter before it goes out. One colleague of mine sent home a newsletter to parents with the intended heading: ASK YOUR CHILD ABOUT. However, the *K* in ASK was accidentally typed as a second *S*. (How's that for a heading?!) This is an embarrassing reminder of how spell-check alone is never enough!

❋ Most principals like to receive a copy of anything that goes home to parents, so, a day or two ahead, pop a copy in your principal's mail box.

The Classroom Web Site

Another communication tool Paula Healey uses with great success is her classroom Web site. A technology buff, Paula created the site herself. It outlines the first grade curriculum, her philosophy of teaching, class rules, and key units. She updates the site every few weeks, adding digital pictures of the children at work and play, along with an information board parents can use for reference. Invite parents with digital cameras to photograph class projects and events. These can be posted on the site as well—a picture is definitely worth a thousand words! (Be sure to get permission from parents before posting students photos on the site.)

Now, granted, not everyone has the interest or the know-how to create their own Web site. But, if you're on a goal-setting cycle, if your school system or continuing education programs offer Web-design training, or if you can barter alternate services with a technophile colleague, you can often learn the basics and create a simple, yet effective Web site. After all, a Web site can be an ongoing work in progress! Strike a deal with your faculty technophile: You create a series of artsy bulletin boards, make up a collection of classroom games, pull together some guided-reading literature collections, visit during your planning periods to conduct sing-alongs, or direct a series of craft activities—and in return you get a Web site! You can check out Paula's Web site at: **www.mrshealeysclass.com.**

The Autumn Open House

Just about every school has an open house evening when parents come for a classroom visit. This may be the first opportunity for many parents to hear, first-hand, about:

- expectations for the grade level,
- curriculum and textbooks,
- scheduling,
- classroom rules and policies,
- homework.

It's important for parents to understand that open house is not a time to confer about individual students but to receive general information. Above all else, this is a time for them to get a sense of who you are, and to see that your classroom will be a positive place for their child. Your school probably has some guidelines explaining what you need to cover during the open house, as well as a school-wide send-home notice that sets the tone, outlines what parents can expect, and provides dates and times for the open house. (Be sure to make yourself familiar with school policies and procedures.)

Open house is the perfect opportunity to share your communication ground rules with parents. I usually hand out a reference sheet for parents called "Keeping in Touch With Mrs. M." This sheet lists office and telephone conference hours, guidelines for effective communication, and an invitation to communicate often. The following is an example of what this reference sheet might look like:

Keeping in Touch With Mrs. M

One important way to provide the best possible education for your child is for you and your child's teacher to stay in touch. I like to communicate often with parents and invite parents to touch base with me as well. If you have a concern, a question, a suggestion, or a comment, I'd love to hear it.

In order to give you my full and undivided attention, I schedule time for conferences and telephone calls throughout the week.

Telephone Calls: You may call and leave me a message here at school any day during school hours. Please leave me your phone number and a detailed message. I return calls between 3:00 and 5:00 P.M. or between 6:00 and 8:30 P.M. I make every effort to get back to you on the day you called.

Conferences: I schedule conferences before and after school on Mondays, Tuesdays, and Thursdays. Please call ahead to schedule a conference. Be sure to explain the nature of the conference and include several times that work for you.

E-mail, Snail-mail: I always welcome notes and letters—electronic or paper! Send a note in with your child or e-mail me from home or work. I return e-mails during breaks in the school day and after 9:00 in the evening. I try to respond to notes and letters the same day. My e-mail address is

_____.

Class Newsletter: At least every other week, our class newsletter will come home. I use the newsletter as a means to keep you informed about units of study, class activities, field trips, homework, and more. Look for the newsletter on Fridays and talk it over with your child.

You can expect to hear from me often, via newsletter, note, e-mail, or phone. I will be in touch with you to share your child's successes, and to discuss any concerns, should they arise.

Sincerely,
Mrs. Mariconda

The Phone Conference

Perhaps the most common parent-teacher communication tool is the telephone. I'll admit that early in my career I dreaded calling parents. It was never easy to deliver information they might be concerned about, worried about, or worse yet, angry and defensive about. Because I anticipated, at worst, a difficult conversation, or at best, a mildly uncomfortable exchange, I often put off making calls. By procrastinating, situations often become more complicated, thus making the dreaded call even more difficult.

However, once my beginning-of-the-year routine included that initial, back-to-school phone call, I had the advantage of getting a feel for each parent's communication style and laying the groundwork for a positive, ongoing relationship. The result was less defensiveness on the part of parents and less hesitancy on my own part.

So, my general rule became: call parents as soon as a concern presents itself. In this way, you can honestly tell parents that you are mildly concerned, that you have a situation you are watching closely, and that you would appreciate their feedback. In turn, parents feel that you are conscientious, that you value their input, and that in your capable, concerned hands, their precious child will not fall through the cracks.

> The back-to-school phone call (page 20) gives you the advantage of getting a feel for each parent's communication style and laying the groundwork for a positive, ongoing relationship. Setting this precedent allows you to follow the most important rule in communicating with parents: *Call parents as soon as a concern presents itself.*

For example, let's imagine that a little girl in your class is having difficulty with spelling and phonics. Her sight vocabulary is adequate, but she struggles when approaching new words that are phonetically predictable. This slows her down when she reads aloud. She also seems nervous and distracted during silent reading time. You're not yet sure if the problem has to do with confidence (she is unwilling to take a chance at sounding out a word) or whether she truly does not have the sound-symbol connection in place. The fact that spelling is difficult seems to point toward a lack of phonemic awareness. You want to discuss this with her parents to see if they have noticed this behavior when reading at home.

From your initial back-to-school phone conversation with the student's parents, you sense that they are a bit nervous, and perhaps, overly concerned about their daughter's performance. You do not want to alarm them, so this information must be presented in a proactive, positive way.

10 Easy Steps To A Successful Phone Conference

1. Open with a greeting and a specific positive comment or light-hearted anecdote.

2. Communicate the reason for your call—a clear explanation of your concern.

3. Offer anecdotal accounts that illustrate your concern. In this way the parent can more clearly understand the situation, based on your observations of the child's behavior. Try to avoid educational buzz words such as *phonemic awareness*, as this kind of terminology may be unfamiliar and, therefore, confusing or threatening to parents. Explain your concern in layman's terms.

4. Tell the parents how you've addressed the situation to date.

5. Ask the parents if they've noticed any similar behaviors.

6. Have an action plan ready to propose to parents.

7. Explain what you plan to do next and when they can expect to hear from you again.

8. Reiterate the ways in which they can contact you.

9. Reassure them that working together, you will be able stay on top of the situation.

10. End with an upbeat, positive goodbye.

Based on this situation, the phone conversation should follow a format such as the ten steps outlined on page 38.

If you find that you're nervous, take some notes prior to making the call. Script the entire conversation if you have to. The last thing you want to do is have the parent sense that you're nervous. Your nervousness may be misinterpreted as defensiveness, anger, frustration, incompetence, or just a sense that the "problem" is much more serious than it really is. If necessary, practice what you'll say—even role play it with a colleague or family member, especially steps 2 and 3 above. Aim for a warm, casual tone of voice.

Here's a sample conversation between a teacher (T) and a student's mother (SM) that follows the ten steps on page 38.

TIP

※ Watch your word choice, as every word we say has certain connotations. Avoid words such as *problem*—use *challenge* instead. Similarly, *concerned* is a less negative term than *worried*.

For more information on choosing your words effectively, see Chapter 5.

Phone Conference Success:

Sample conversation

T: Hi, Mrs. Wauthier?

SM: Yes?

T: It's Barbara Mariconda, Sara's teacher.

SM: Hi, Mrs. Mariconda. How are you?

T: I'm good, thanks. School's been great—we've really been enjoying our unit on the Native Americans of the Southwest. We've been doing a number of related art projects that Sara really enjoys. She did the most amazing chalk piece of a pueblo village.

SM: She told us all about it. We can't wait to see the bulletin board.

T: Stop by any time. . . . Do you have a few minutes to chat? I'd like to brainstorm a little with you about Sara's work in spelling and in sounding out new vocabulary.

SM: Absolutely. We make sure she studies for her spelling test for at least a half an hour on Thursday nights. She works on it, but she still just can't remember some of the words. Should we be spending more time?

T: I don't think so. It sounds like you're doing fine. But I've noticed that "sounding out" is sometimes challenging for Sara. For example, she was writing a title for her desert animal picture The Kit Fox, and she couldn't decide which vowels to use. She wound up writing The C-e-t F-a-x. She really tried hard to sound out those basic short vowels—the ones our weekly spelling list has been focusing on—but she still found it difficult.

Continued on next page

SM: Do the other kids have as much trouble with this?

T: Well, spelling presents a number of different challenges for different students. Some can sound out with little difficulty, but struggle with sight words, which are words that aren't spelled the way they sound and therefore must be memorized—for example, words like *the, want,* or *does.* Sara does well memorizing many of these sight words, but she struggles a bit when approaching new words that could be sounded out.

SM: Do you think she has a learning disability or a real problem?

T: This kind of thing simply can be developmental, meaning that as she matures the sounding-out skills will fall into place. It's the kind of thing I want to watch closely in order to monitor her progress over time. I've been making it a point to reinforce the sounding-out skills when we work in small groups during reading. I'll continue to do this, and I thought it might be helpful to have our reading specialist come into the classroom to observe Sara. She might have some fun games and practice activities that can help boost these skills.

SM: That sounds good. But should we be worried about this? What can we do to help?

T: I wouldn't worry about this at all. As I said, I'll continue to monitor Sara's progress, and when Ms. Coe, our reading specialist comes in, she might offer some additional insights. In the meantime, I have some workbook materials and a phonics card game that most children enjoy. I thought that maybe you could have some fun with it at home. The key is to keep it light. We don't want Sara to become concerned or self-conscious. If you'd like, you could stop by after school some day this week and I can introduce you and Sara to the materials.

SM: How about Thursday when I pick her up?

T: Terrific! And when you come you can see that bulletin board!

SM: Wonderful!

T: Okay, Mrs. Wauthier, it was great talking to you. I'll see you on Thursday after school, from 3:35–4:00. In the meantime, I'll invite Ms. Coe in. I'd expect that she'll stop by to observe sometime next week. After that, I'll give you a call— definitely by next Friday.

SM: Thank you so much. I really appreciate your concern!

T: Thank you, Mrs. Wauthier. And remember, you can call or e-mail me anytime. I'll see you on Thursday!

SM: Great. Goodbye.

T: Bye.

It's a good idea to maintain a communication log to keep track of each call and conference, note what was discussed, and list any necessary follow-up. (See the reproducible planning template on pages 67 and 68 and strategies for organizing a communication binder on page 25.)

Classroom Conferences

There are times when a face-to-face parent conference is preferable to a phone call. A conference affords you the opportunity to share actual samples of student work and to include other staff members: the reading specialist, school psychologist, or even last year's teacher. Asking parents to attend a conference in person implies that the issue requires serious attention. If you have had several phone conversations with parents and the issue has not been resolved, a parent conference is the next logical step.

Parents might also wish to call a conference. Therefore, having regularly scheduled office hours is a must. Remember, you do not want to get caught "on the fly" by a parent before or after school. Instead, you want time to think about the situation, plan what you need to communicate, decide who to include, gather together any relevant work samples or test data, and come up with a tentative action plan.

But, why have regular office hours? Why not simply schedule conferences on an as-needed basis?

The reason is that teaching is much more than a full-time job, and if you're not careful, the teaching, planning, correcting, phoning, and conferring can take over your entire life. It's important to schedule your own personal or family time and stick to it. Otherwise there will always be something to plan, tests to correct, parents to meet, and soon you'll have no family or personal time left. So, if you take your daughter to her piano lesson on Tuesdays, and on Thursdays the two of you go to the mall, stick to that. Offer before-school conference times on those days, and perhaps an after-school hour on another day. I recommend before-school conferences because you can better control the amount of time you spend. Having exactly 45 minutes before the first bell will guarantee that the exchange is concise and productive, and that it draws to a close on time.

Most issues, both academic and behavioral, usually can be addressed successfully at a parent conference. However, if you suspect that the issue may run deeper, perhaps indicating a potential learning disability, or an ongoing emotional or behavioral issue, then testing or intervention from the school psychologist may be in order. Be sure to mention this at the conference as a future possibility.

Keep in mind that terms like learning disability, school psychologist, and planning and placement team meeting (PPT) can sound extremely serious and threatening to parents. Always refer to testing as simply a means to gain information that can help address the needs of the child, and the school psychologist as a valuable resource for successfully dealing with a whole range of needs of school-age children. I always make these references matter-of-factly and stress that these are resources that countless parents and students have taken advantage of.

10 Quick Tips
For a Successful
Parent Conference

1. "Prep" the parents for the conference. Make sure you have spoken to the parents beforehand about the issue and that they understand the issue has been addressed through a number of strategies. The conference is not the time to drop a bombshell; it is a time to further explore an issue or ongoing concern.

2. Be clear about what you want to accomplish and have an outcome in mind. For example, share samples of work, present three strategies to address the concern, and brainstorm with parents about at-home follow-through.

3. As in the phone conference, always present anecdotal accounts that illustrate your concern. In this way, the parent can more clearly understand the situation, based on your observations of the child's behavior. Try to avoid buzz words such as *phonemic awareness*, as this kind of terminology may be unfamiliar and therefore threatening to parents. Explain your concern in layman's terms.

4. Tell the parents how you've addressed the situation to date.

5. Carefully watch facial expressions and body language so you can gauge any "hotspots" and respond sensitively.

6. Ask the parents about their observations and how they think you can be most helpful.

7. Have an action plan ready to propose to parents.

8. Explain what you plan to do next and when they can expect to hear from you again.

9. Reiterate the ways in which they may contact you.

10. Reassure them that by working together, you will be able to stay on top of the situation and end with an upbeat, positive goodbye.

DEALING EFFECTIVELY WITH AN ANGRY PARENT DURING A CONFERENCE

Should parents become upset, angry, or defensive during a conference it's essential to stay calm and cool. It's important to remember that they are, first and foremost, concerned about their child, that this concern may be expressed emotionally, and that anxiety may be displaced onto the teacher.

> Remember that parents are first and foremost, concerned about their child, that this concern may be expressed emotionally, and that anxiety may be displaced onto the teacher.

How do you address an angry or distraught parent? Imagine that during a conference at which you recommend testing, a mother begins to cry, and then raises her voice at you:

> "I don't understand this. Last year this wasn't a problem at all. She didn't have this much trouble in first grade! Now you want to have her tested?"

Following are some "tension busters"—strategies for defusing tension when it arises during a conference. (See Chapter Four for an extended discussion of ways to build trust and defuse negative emotions.)

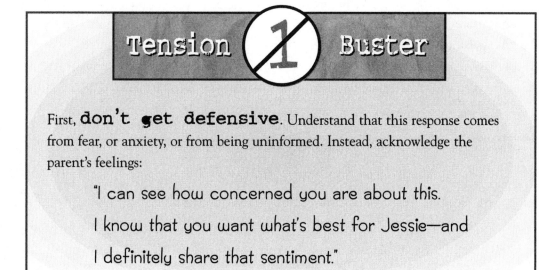

Tension 1 Buster

First, **don't get defensive**. Understand that this response comes from fear, or anxiety, or from being uninformed. Instead, acknowledge the parent's feelings:

> "I can see how concerned you are about this. I know that you want what's best for Jessie—and I definitely share that sentiment."

Tension Buster

By referring to the outburst as concern, you avoid any negative judgment. You **affirm that you understand** the level to which the parent cares for her child no matter how she expresses that concern, and you open the door for the parent to enter back into a productive conversation. A calm, even tone of voice, combined with direct eye contact is best. Never tell parents there is nothing to be upset about—this negates their feelings. Instead, try gently to steer the conversation back to the issues:

> "Let's back up for a moment and look at this again," or "How do you think I can be most helpful?"

Tension Buster

Don't suggest strategies that are unlikely to take place. For example, if you know that the parent works two jobs and does not have a good track record on follow-through with homework or discipline, suggesting a home component (which in a perfect world would seem reasonable) will only frustrate everyone concerned and create more problems. Remember that **each situation is different** and may require a creative and unique response.

Tension Buster

I've also found that **sharing personal anecdotes** with distraught parents can go a long way in lowering their anxiety. For example, if a mother is upset about the possibility of having her child receive "special education" or "resource room" support, you could casually mention how such support helped your nephew (who recently graduated from Brown University) with his early reading problems—how it built up his confidence and eventually eliminated his resistance to completing work on his own. Or you could share an anecdote about how a behavior modification program (which you might refer to as an "incentive plan") of sticker cards helped your own daughter attend better to what was happening in the classroom and stay on task.

In this way, parents can clearly see that you are not in any way judging their child or their parenting skills, or viewing any special services as out of the ordinary. Don't have a nephew or daughter? Talk about past success stories of anonymous students you've had in the past.

These strategies can get parents off the defensive and back to dealing with the issue. After presenting some objective data (test scores, student work, anecdotal accounts, the observations of other professionals), asking parents what they would like to see happen can be both revealing and helpful.

Of course, one of the best ways to prevent tense exchanges is to build up relationships with parents during the course of the year when things are going well. If solid, trust-filled relationships already exist, it is so much easier to handle exchanges that might otherwise be tricky. A great, often-overlooked tool for building strong relationships is parent volunteering.

Making the Most of Parent Volunteers

When I first began teaching second grade, I faced a management challenge. I wanted to use learning stations as a means of providing small group, hands-on instruction. Organizing math manipulatives, conducting science experiments, and coordinating social studies–related art projects required another pair (or two) of adult hands. But, there were no extra hands to be had—unless I invited parents in to help.

The idea frightened me a little. I didn't want a child twho misbehaved or a project that flopped to reflect poorly on me. In short, I didn't want them to judge me or find me lacking. It was safer, with the challenging group of youngsters I had that year, not to have parents in.

Eventually it occurred to me that parents might feel the same way every time their child walked through my door—that I was judging their parenting based on the child's behavior. Yet, they sent the child to school every day! I realized that inviting them to volunteer built a bridge of trust that led to mutual respect.

I sent home a notice explaining the objectives for learning stations and the times I needed coverage. Many parents enthusiastically signed up and agreed to attend a mandatory meeting. The meeting and the resulting participation proved to be a huge success and I've followed a similar meeting structure every year.

THE VOLUNTEER ORIENTATION MEETING

At the orientation meeting, I explain that parents' help will be beneficial in the following ways. Parent volunteers

- ❋ allow the class to do more complicated, high-interest activities, such as hands-on center work.

- ❋ facilitate small-group activities that require supervision.

- ❋ offer children the opportunity to interact positively with a variety of adult leaders.

- ❋ enjoy a first-hand experience, where they can learn about their children's social environment and the curriculum.

Then I pass out a list of the class rules and some simple tips on keeping children engaged and on task (tips about positive reinforcement and redirecting off-task and negative behaviors, and a set of guidelines for knowing when to call on the teacher to intervene). Finally, I discuss the classroom confidentiality rule with them. I acknowledge that everyone in the class, adults included, has good days and not-so-good days. I make it a point to keep classroom issues inside the classroom and I ask parents to do the same. While I expect them to report any negative or problematic behaviors to me, I also insist that they avoid discussing another child's behavior outside of the classroom.

I send out a volunteer schedule ahead of time, and the day before each lesson that involves parent assistance, I send a simple lesson plan home to parent volunteers so they can be prepared.

A well-organized volunteer system helps parents feel involved and helps them better understand and teach their kids. Futhermore, parents who spend time in the classroom come away with a renewed respect for what you do and will do almost anything to support you! These parents become your advocates, your personal PR reps, and your biggest fans. They begin to see, first-hand, the multi-tasking, complex planning, and real skill it takes to run a classroom. The most common comment I received was, "Wow, I don't know how you do it!"

I really encourage you to invite parents in. Whether it's for learning stations, read alouds, or as assistants for special projects, have them come in. Do take note of the quick tips on the next page to make the most of their participation.

Remember, the key to implementing the communication vehicles highlighted in this chapter—the weekly or biweekly newsletter, e-mail newsletter, classroom Web site, autumn open house, phone conferences, parent conferences, and classroom volunteers— is to plan well, always be prepared, and to choose several that you use on a regular basis, until each one becomes second nature! Like anything else you do, practicing your communication skills makes your interactions with parents, if not perfect, certainly more comfortable and effective! And parents will thank you, too!

5 Quick Tips for Implementing & Managing Parent Volunteers

1. Meet with parents first to share management tips, redirection techniques, and the confidentiality rule.

2. Make a schedule and stick to it. Give parents plenty of advance notice and clear, concise plans for their volunteer time.

3. Communicate exactly what parents are going to do and what roles they will play. Avoid having parents regularly plan a craft activity or project, as they usually do not have the class management skills to ensure that it will run smoothly. You, the teacher, must be responsible for the planning and the underlying management.

4. Be watchful and supportive of parents, always ready to step in and handle a challenging situation. Also, be ready to intervene if a parent is speaking or redirecting a student in an inappropriate or ineffective manner.

5. Thank parents often for their help. An end-of-the-year tea or breakfast is a lovely gesture of appreciation.

Chapter 4

Communication Techniques

for Defusing Tension

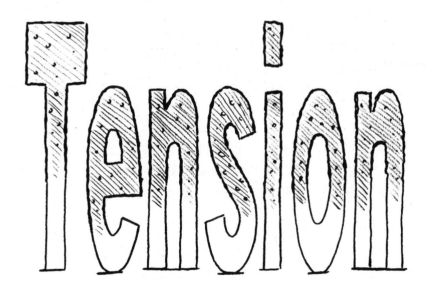

I can't think of anyone who enjoys dealing with a potentially sensitive, touchy, or negative issue. Yet, as educators, this is a reality of the job. As I discussed in the section on classroon conferences in Chapter Three, parents' anxiety can create real tension. No matter how much care you put into setting the stage for successful communication with parents, there will be times when you have to address concerns or issues that you know will make parents feel uncomfortable, upset, or even angry. There will be times when you need to listen not only to parents' concerns, but also to their complaints and criticism.

Whether you are writing a note home, returning a phone call or e-mail, or requesting a conference, you should have a range of techniques for defusing tension in order to promote a positive outcome.

I discovered many such techniques while working on my Master's Degree in Communication. At first, I was less than excited about classes with titles like: "Systems and Theories of Human Communication," "Negotiation," and "Advertising and Public Opinion" and wondered about their relevance to my teaching. And, once I began, I found I was the only teacher in the program. The majority of the other students were executives and middle managers from the corporate world.

You can imagine how delighted I was to find that much of this "boring" coursework touched on issues relevant to teaching. In fact, I began to see just how sketchy my undergraduate work in education was in preparing me for the kind of interactions I had to face with parents day in and day out.

Five Key Techniques to Create Trust and Respect in Every Situation

I discovered five surefire underlying rules for establishing mutual trust and respect in any communication with parents. We'll look at each of these in practical terms.

IN EVERY CONVERSATION, NOTE, OR CONFERENCE:

1. Show a genuine concern and respect for the parent's point of view.

2. Practice active listening in order to discover the wants and needs of the other.

3. Focus on improvement, not judgment. Be careful not to criticize or blame (watch what your words imply).

4. Strive to exceed parents' expectations in terms of your response.

5. Set incremental goals that are clear and measurable.

1. **Show a genuine concern and respect for the parent's point of view.** A friend of mine, a particularly anxious mother of an active little boy, told me about a conference she'd called with her son's teacher. She was concerned about her son's apparent lack of interest in reading.

When she expressed her concern, the teacher pointed out that her son had earned a reading grade of a "B" on his last report card, and that he completed all his work on time, although he was sometimes careless. The teacher ended with a comment like, "He's doing fine, I don't know what you're so worried about." The entire exchange did little to ease the mother's anxiety, and she came away from the conference feeling as though she'd been foolish to have brought it up at all.

This is an example in which the teacher did not really acknowledge the other's point of view. He minimized the mother's concern, which was not about her son's reading grade; rather, it was about his seeming lack of interest in reading. In fact, the teacher simply reiterated information that the mother already knew, thus making the conference seem like a waste of time.

In talking with my friend about her little boy and looking at his work folder, it was clear that his skills in both phonemic awareness and comprehension were solid, and that he did an adequate job of completing related independent work. (Exactly what the report card and the teacher's comments reflected.) However, I observed that he was an extremely active child, with a somewhat short attention span. I could easily see, based on the teacher's comments, how he might rush through his work in order to move on to other activities.

My guess is that this teacher had many other students facing greater challenges in reading than my friend's son, and with this in mind, my friend's youngster presented little cause for concern. But that was not the issue for this mother. The teacher did not hear what she was saying, and did not respect her point of view in regard to his lack of interest in reading.

This conference would have had a much more positive outcome if the teacher had:

❄ **reiterated the parent's concern.** *It's essential for the teacher to be clear about the parent's real issue. Whether or not the teacher shares the concern is secondary. The parent needs to know that he or she has been heard. A simple response could accomplish this. For example, "What I hear you saying is that while Johnny is doing satisfactory work in reading, he doesn't seem to take much interest in reading recreationally." Then wait for the parent to confirm, reiterate, or clarify.*

※ **asked questions.** *"What have you observed at home that leads you to think Johnny isn't interested in reading?" is a question I would have asked. Perhaps the parent would explain that Johnny only reads the same simple books over and over again, and resists reading books that seem to be more on his grade level. This is good information, because then the teacher could explain that most of us, adults included, read material well below our reading ability level for recreational purposes. In fact, many adult magazines are written at about a sixth-grade level—perfect for light browsing in your doctor's waiting room or for a quick read with a cup of coffee mid-morning. This "revelation" would go a long way in easing the parent's concern.*

※ **determined the parent's primary concern.** *Is the parent afraid that the apparent lack of interest reflects a lack of skill or confidence? Is the parent concerned that this lack of interest signals a poor attitude, which could be related to some other behavioral issues at home or at school? Is the parent concerned because her child has also lost interest in Cub Scouts, karate lessons, and even T.V., and that he or she might be depressed. It's clear that being sensitive to the other's point of view by gently exploring their concerns can lead to a much more productive meeting for all involved.*

Let's look a little closer at the role of listening and questioning as a means of learning more about the other's concern.

2. **Practice active listening.** Many times we know someone hears our words, but we aren't all that certain that they actually "get it." Active listening is a technique that affirms the speaker and encourages him or her to continue to open up and share. There are a number of simple components that make up active listening and all of them send a clear message to the speaker: "I'm with you; I'm interested in what you have to say; I understand you; and I want to learn more." Bill Makahilahila, Director of Human Resources at SCS-Thomson Microelectronics says, "A person who is actively listening is usually the one who is asking questions and then waiting for a response as opposed to coming up with an instant solution." By actively listening you can usually uncover the underlying concern, oftentimes something the parent may not be able initially to pinpoint or name. By helping the parent first clarify and express the entire scope of their own concerns, and then address those concerns directly, you become a strong ally.

Here are some "affirming" phrases you can use to assure parents that you're listening:

Yes, I see.

I understand.

What I hear you saying is that . . .

So, let me be sure that I understand. You're concerned that . . .

I can see why you feel that way.

Of course.

Tell me a little more.

I'm so glad you're sharing this.

Your observations are really helpful.

I've noticed that as well.

I think you're right about that.

I do appreciate your candor.

It's very helpful for me to get a sense of the whole picture.

These comments encourage parents to go on, to reveal their worries, observations, wants, and needs. But sometimes comments aren't enough. The teacher needs to do some questioning in order to get a more comprehensive understanding of the situation.

Here are some general questions that can be helpful in a variety of situations:

What are you most concerned about?

Can you give me a specific example of what you mean?

When did you first become concerned about/aware of this?

Do you notice any similar behaviors at home?

What do you think is working well for your child right now?

What would you like to see happen?

How can I be most helpful right now?

These questions can reveal quite a lot about what parents worry about and what they want. Once you know what they're worried about, you can directly address these concerns. Once you know what they want, you can begin to put a plan in place. Even if what the parents want (e.g., "We don't want her going to the resource room for reading, we want her to stay with her class") does not match with what you feel is in the best interest of the child, at least you know where the parent is coming from and can build your professional case for the child's best interest with the parent's perspective in mind. You'll have a better sense of the concerns you need to address and the issues you need to deal with. In his book *The Leader in You* (Simon & Schuster, 1993), Dale Carnegie writes, "Nobody is more persuasive than a good listener."

3. **Focus on improvement, not judgment** (i.e., make criticism constructive). You've had a trying week, jammed with cumbersome class projects, meetings, phone calls, and testing. You lost two hours due to a snow delay, and your planning period went south because the music teacher was absent. Your classroom is littered with the remains of this afternoon's art project, and report cards and parent conferences are just days away. Top that off with a call from your son's school—he isn't feeling well and needs to go home. You wait your turn for the office phone, call your mother, your spouse, and your next-door neighbor to see if someone can pick up your ailing son and watch him until you get home.

The final bells rings, and you're making a beeline for the door, when a parent stops you in your tracks. And, based on the way your day has gone, you're not surprised when she hits you with a complaint. She's unhappy, feels you've treated her son unfairly, and wants to talk with you about it—now. Before you can even explain that you have a sick child at the neighbor's house and have to leave immediately, she's blurted out the whole issue: He's been deprived of his recess three times in the last several weeks, the other kids blame him for things he didn't do, and you pick on him when other kids get away with the same kinds of behavior. So, what are you going to do about it?

Her criticism is just about enough to put you over the edge. You feel angry, defensive, and unjustly accused. You'd like to tell her that her son is a handful, doesn't follow the rules, and has received the consequences he's deserved, and maybe with consistent follow-through at home, he'd learn a little self-control. Of course, you hold your tongue. But, what is the best response to criticism, however unfair it may seem?

There are a number of steps to take in processing criticism and defusing tension in order to move toward positive outcomes. Here are a few tips to keep in mind.

10 Quick Tips to Communicate Constructively & Defuse Tension

1. **Initially, simply acknowledge the parent's criticism.** "I can see how upset you are about this, and it's important for me to explore this with you thoroughly so that we can address the situation."

2. **If possible, schedule a meeting for another time.** "I want to give you my full attention on this, so let's schedule a meeting when we won't be interrupted." This also gives you time to sort out the situation, consider your response, and have a plan of action ready to propose.

3. **Hear the parent out, without interruption.** Though the parent may be making assumptions based on partial or false information, let the parent vent. Listen actively to learn, and then recap, the parent's issue to be sure you understand his or her position.

4. **Put yourself in the parent's shoes.** Remember that a parent's primary interest is in his or her child, and that the parent is acting out of love and concern. This allows you to let go of some of your natural defensiveness.

5. **Move from generalizations toward specific instances.** When the parent states, "You always pick on him," ask for a specific instance, instead of jumping in to defend yourself. "I'm glad you brought that up. It's important that we look at this together. Can you tell me about a specific time when Johnny felt I was singling him out?" This opens the door for an objective conversation about a specific instance and allows the parent to begin to see the situation from your perspective. You can then provide a first-hand account of the incident in objective, non-judgmental terms.

6. **Try to keep your language objective to avoid making judgments about the student's character.** Stick to clear-cut phrases like, *"I saw Johnny punch Russell,"* or *"I heard the boys shouting at one another,"* rather than a more subjective statement like, *"He was being aggressive and was really out of control."*

7. **Explain how your behavior/response/strategy was intended to benefit the child.** A parent complains because you removed her son from

Continued on next page

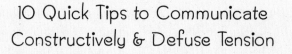

the group during a hands-on science experiment. "You're right, Danny was excited about the experiment, and I do love his enthusiasm. Still, primarily, I was concerned about his safety. He was very excited and went ahead instead of waiting for directions. He mishandled and broke a glass slide, endangering himself and others. So, I asked him to take five minutes to listen to the directions without the distraction of the materials in front of him. When I felt certain he'd heard the directions I asked him to rejoin the group." Be ready to explain why your policy is what it is, why you assigned that huge project, why you moved Anna's seat, or why you kept Allison in during recess. The reason should always be related to the best interest of that child and all the children in the classroom.

8. **If you were wrong, admit it.** Nothing disarms an angry person faster than an acknowledgment that you were wrong. "I can really see that from a different perspective now. I think you are absolutely right about this. It seems there was more to the incident than met the eye, and I jumped to an unfortunate conclusion. I'm so glad you took the time to discuss it with me. Now I can go ahead and correct the situation."

9. **Don't shift the blame to the parent.** It's easy, when you feel under attack, to retaliate, even in subtle ways. "He'd really benefit from an incentive program like this at home—it would definitely help with his self-control." However, what parents hear is the implication that they're not doing their job. (And, even if they're not, defensive parents will not be open to suggestions or to constructive criticism.) Instead, ask: "Have you noticed any of these behaviors at home?" From there you can enlist their help. "We might even consider extending this incentive program at home as well. I'll bet Jason would really benefit from the consistency it would provide."

10. **Build on what is working.** A parent tells you that her daughter Jess is bored during math. You feel that the child is using this as an excuse to avoid class work that is suddenly challenging. Instead of debating whether or not math is boring, ask the parent what aspects of the school day seem stimulating for the child. Let's say the parent responds that the learning stations in which students work in small cooperative groups seem to work for Jess. Make it a point to try this approach during math. After all, it's also an opportunity for you to work with her in a small group to tackle the challenging material—and as long as math begins to work for Jess, every-one will be happy!

4. **Strive to exceed parents' expectations.** Go beyond what is expected in terms of your response. Always ask yourself what the parents need in order to feel that the issue was resolved satisfactorily. Then, whenever possible, give them a little more. Let's assume that Marianna's mother asserts that you have not been attentive to the fact that Marianna is still struggling with basic math facts. She demands an at-home program so that at least somebody will provide extra practice. You hear the implication: *Since the school isn't doing it, I'll have to do it myself.* Your position is that Marianna conceptually understands addition and subtraction—she just has not yet committed the facts to memory, which doesn't concern you, since that isn't an educational objective right now. However, instead of defending yourself, explain the objective, acknowledge that eventually it is important to have math facts handy, and then share the kinds of hands-on activities that you've been doing in school. Thank the mother for her interest and give her copies of some appropriate math games and activities.

Then, take it a step further. To be certain that Marianna is where she needs to be, arrange several before- or after-school sessions with her for some additional work. Place a call to Marianna's home after each of these meetings to offer reassurance. Marianna's mother will receive valuable information and feedback—in fact, more than she requested—and most important, she will feel heard.

5. **Set incremental goals that are clear and measurable.** You meet with a parent to set up a behavior-modification plan for a student with ADD (Attention Deficit Disorder). The parent requests a weekly report to see if there is any improvement. The parent wants the child's special weekend activities and privileges to be a reward for "good" behavior and progress. Sounds like a reasonable plan, but it will definitely flop unless you all share an objective, measurable definition of "good behavior."

For example, if the child can earn a sticker for each 45 minute block of on-task activity, a reasonable initial goal might be 4 out of 6 stickers a day, 3 out of 5 days a week. This is objective and measurable. After the child has internalized more self-control for longer periods of time, the goal might increase to 5 out of 6 stickers a day, 3 out of 5 days a week, then 3 out of 5 a day, 4 out of 6 days a week. Sending a tally sheet home at the end of each week is more valuable than a note stating that the child had a "good" week or a "bad" week.

Whether the issue is behavior, sight vocabulary, math facts, or any number of other issues, setting measurable, incremental goals provides

◎ a record of the child's progress.

◎ objective data for further conversations with parents.

- benchmarks for growth.
- the means to break large goals into manageable chunks.
- more frequent opportunities to share the student's success and offer positive feedback.

Securing Support From Your Principal

It is critical to gain not only the support of parents, but of your school's principal as well. Many an angry parent has gone right over a teacher's head to vent directly to the principal. For this reason, whenever I sense that a parent seems tense, unhappy, or angry, I present the situation to my principal—well before the parent approaches her. I outline what communications  I've shared with the parents, any pertinent background information about the situation, and my overall impression of what the issues are for the parent. In this way, if the parent were to go over my head, the principal would be in a better position to respond appropriately and be supportive of me. Always keep in mind that principals like being surprised about as much as parents and teachers do—so make it your business to keep them posted on potentially sensitive situations with parents.

Using these techniques can successfully defuse tension, promote mutual respect, and transform judgment into positive change, all of which will ultimately benefit the child. Practice the techniques often and you'll notice something else: Not only will parents' tension, anxiety, anger, and defensiveness melt away—so will yours!

Chapter 5

The Power of Words

positive responses

WORDS 101

connotations

communication

literal meanings

Words carry a great deal of power. When a teacher speaks to a parent, the words, of course, carry a literal meaning. But, parents will hear and process a lot more than the literal meaning. Words also carry connotation, forming an unspoken, yet extremely powerful subtext within an exchange.

Case in point: When my wonderful, marvelous, talented, sweet, creative, intelligent daughter was in the second grade, I attended my first parent conference with her teacher. After a moment or two of pleasantries, I asked how my daughter was doing. I will never forget the teacher's response: "Well," she said, "fine, but she has no confidence." (Hence a cardinal rule of mine—*Fine* and *but* do not belong in the same sentence. Let the positive stand on its own.) My response to the teacher was something articulate, something like, "She has no confidence?"

My daughter was a little shy in new situations, but I wouldn't call that "no confidence." I'd call that cautious. I'd call it observant. I'd call it judicious, circumspect, watchful. But no confidence? I sat listening to a list of all the ways in which my daughter demonstrated her lack of confidence, trying to keep my natural defensiveness under control. (There were no specific examples, by the way, of the "fine" part of the report. A big mistake.) By the end of the list—". . . she has to come up to my desk to ask questions about every assignment, she insists on showing me her work before she completes it . . ."—I was doing a slow burn. Because what I saw immediately was that after having two "warm and fuzzy" teachers in previous years, teachers who dished out positive reinforcement like it was going out of style, my little one was experiencing culture shock. She was simply looking for affirmation. I stopped the teacher mid-stream (she hadn't paused to ask me for my take on the situation, but I was certainly going to

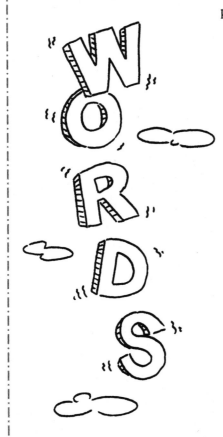

provide it!) and asked her point blank, "Have you ever given her an alternative strategy for checking her work? Have you told her that you value working independently? Have you given her a little positive feedback when she has worked well independently?" And yes, I admit, I fired those questions at her—I couldn't help it. Fortunately, my questions were the questions of a seasoned educator, but that same defensiveness might have translated into a personal verbal attack coming from a parent less schooled in the ins and outs of classroom dynamics.

How different the tone of our exchange might have been had the teacher chosen her words more carefully. She could have said, "Marissa is a cautious, observant child who appreciates reinforcement in new situations. We're working on some strategies to help her work more independently with confidence." While the meaning may be basically the same, the connotation of "she has no confidence" is so different. It focuses on the negative and negates the positive, while the alternative focuses on the child's attributes that can be viewed in a positive way. It also points toward a goal. The comment, "We're working on some strategies . . ." suggests the teacher believes that growth will take place, rather than the definitive and rather hopeless pronouncement, "She has no confidence." The connotation is completely different.

In this chapter, we'll look at a range of "challenging" ideas that a teacher might need to express. We'll consider both the literal meaning and the connotation, and most important, offer alternatives for words or phrases that carry this kind of damaging negative energy. You can use the simple reference charts that follow to evaluate often-used comments for their literal meaning and potentially negative connotation, and then check out an alternate choice of words that address the issue in a more positive way. Notice that the alternate choice of words often begins with a positive observation and involves an objective report, carefully avoiding the subjective "labeling language" in the literal example. These "Better Said" ideas focus on what is in the best interest of the child. We'll also look at positive responses to some of the negative verbal messages that may be directed at you by parents.

Common Responses for Conferences, Report Cards, and More:

Literal Meanings, Connotative Implications

The charts that follow on pages 62–65 show how common words and phrases that teachers and parents use to express concerns can be loaded with negative—and usually unintended—meanings. The first two charts evaluate teacher comments about academic and behavioral concerns that send the wrong message to parents. Notice that in the "Literal Meaning" column, the emphasis is on the problem, with little evidence of an improvement plan. The connotation, described in the second column, is extremely negative. In the "Better Said" column the emphasis is on objective observation, an attitude of concern, and when appropriate, a tentative improvement plan.

If you find yourself on the receiving end of an emotional exchange, it's critical to know how to defuse the tension and to be as objective as possible. The third chart, "When Parents Vent," evaluates emotionally-charged remarks made by worried, upset parents to teachers and offers suggestions for appropriate responses. Each exchange includes a critical remark from the parent, the teacher's gut reaction (the "knee-jerk" response you'd like to blurt out), and finally, a translation of that response into an appropriate, positive tool for improvement. As the professional, the teacher's job is to get a clear understanding of the situation and the parent's point of view, without taking it personally, and guide the conver-sation back to the best interest of the child. (See 10 Quick Tips to Communicate Constructively and Defuse Tension on pages 55 and 56 for a review of how to handle a difficult conversation with a parent.)

Suggestion

Use ideas from the "Better Said" column on pages 62 and 63 to help you phrase report card comments about academic and behavioral concerns.

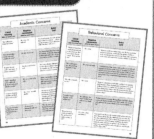

Academic Concerns

Literal Meaning *(What the teacher says)*	Negative connotation *(What the parent hears)*	Better Said
"She's falling way behind in reading."	*She's slow—she might fail.*	"I've been keeping close tabs on Jane's reading. Here's what I've noticed . . . (Show samples, cite specific instances.) Let's talk about some strategies for addressing these skill areas."
"Dan's been fooling around, and won't complete his work."	*He's lazy, doesn't care.*	"I've noticed lately that Dan seems a little distracted. For example, on Monday during math time, we were working with unifix cubes. He knocked over Jason's tower, and was unable to complete his own."
"Joannie's become careless and sloppy on written assignments."	*She takes no pride in her work.*	"I've seen a distinct difference in Joannie's work lately. Look at these reading assignments: This one is from two months ago, this one from last month. Here's what I've seen most recently."
"John's comprehension is really weak—he doesn't understand what he's reading."	*He's not as smart as the others.*	"John's oral reading is really fluent and smooth. What I want to focus on now are comprehension skills and strategies to help him thoroughly understand what he's reading."
"I suspect a learning disability and think Katie needs testing."	*She's "slow," mentally disabled.*	"It seems to me that we'll need some more information about the way Katie learns in order to better meet her needs in the classroom. These tests will reveal her strengths and will break open the puzzle of what she finds challenging so that we can present these skills in a manner that is most advantageous."
"I'm sure you realize Robbie hasn't done his homework in a week."	*The parent isn't following through and doesn't care.*	"I'm sure you're unaware that I haven't received any homework from Robbie this week. I'm concerned about this and want to explore what we can do together to help him meet this requirement."

Behavioral Concerns

Literal Meaning (What the teacher says)	Negative connotation (What the parent hears)	Better Said
"Shannon's been bossy on the playground and in the classroom. She's got to learn that she cannot always get her way."	*She's a brat.*	"Shannon really has a mind of her own. She has good ideas and strong opinions—real leadership qualities. I'd like to work on tempering her conviction in things with a sensitivity to the wants and needs of less assertive children in the class."
"He's really aggressive. He can't keep his hands to himself."	*He's mean and angry.*	"On Wednesday Marc got in a fight on the soccer field and punched another boy in the stomach. Yesterday he kicked a girl who got in front of him in the bus line. I'd like us to put our heads together to see how we can help Marc with some more positive ways to deal with disappointments and frustrations."
"She talks constantly in class."	*She's a pest.*	"Jessica is a gregarious, social child—and she's very popular with her peers. Often, she finds quiet work time to be a real challenge. I'd love to explore ways in which we can help Jessica during these times so that she doesn't become distracted from her learning, and so that she doesn't inadvertently distract others."
"I caught Crystal cheating on her spelling test."	*She's dishonest. You haven't instilled strong values in your daughter.*	"I think Crystal is worrying about spelling. Last Friday during our test she had her wordlist in her lap. I quietly took it away and explained why using it during a test was not helpful or fair."
"Wayne has been caught in numerous lies, and has been caught stealing, as well."	*He's a liar, a thief, and dishonest.*	"Last week I saw Wayne take another child's gel-pen from his desk. Wayne told me that the child had given it to him, but the other child denied it. We've talked about respecting others' personal space and belongings, and Wayne decided to return the items and write an apology. I also feel that we need to set some boundaries and consequences, and thought you'd be able to help."

When Parents Vent

Literal Meaning (What the parent says)	Negative connotation (What the teacher feels)	Appropriate Response
"You've let him fail! He is devastated!"	*I gave you and him fair warning, did the best I could, and you all preferred to ignore it.*	"I am as frustrated as you are about this. Especially after we reviewed his test grades and discussed his average at midterm. I'm sure this will be a good opportunity for Brad to take seriously the responsibility for completing his independent assignments and preparing for tests. He is very bright, and I'm confident that together we can put an incentive plan in place that will both encourage him to complete work, and that eventually will demonstrate the satisfaction that can come from doing things well on his own."
"I don't want her sitting near that girl. She's always causing trouble and you blame Missy. I'm sick of it."	*No matter where she sits there's a problem. You just don't want to deal with it—it's easier to blame someone else.*	"I'm so sorry you feel that Missy has been unfairly blamed. Why don't the three of us sit down together and discuss this? That way we can clear the air and be sure that we're all on the same wavelength about the class rules and consequences. We can also figure out a seating arrangement that will be best for all of the students."
"You've given Jason a detention three days this month. He's missed his study hall and he's missed basketball. If you could control the class better, maybe he'd behave."	*If he followed the rules there wouldn't be a problem. If you were supportive instead of making excuses, maybe he'd shape up.*	"It sounds as though you're concerned about the behavior of students in class and that you're worried about control in the classroom. I'd love to be able to set your mind at ease on this issue—why not come in and observe a class? Our class rules, as well as consequences for not following them, are posted and I think it would be valuable for you to see the way in which I implement these procedures. It also sounds as though study hall and basketball are important to Jason. After your visit I'd be happy to get together to discuss how we can help Jason avoid these consequences in the future."

When Parents Vent

Literal Meaning (What the parent says)	Negative connotation (What the teacher feels)	Appropriate Response
"I don't understand this problem in reading all of a sudden. It certainly wasn't a problem last year in Mrs. Cannon's class."	*So, the problem is that I don't teach as well as Mrs. Cannon.*	"You're right. I've reviewed his file from last year and I see that his reading assessments and grades were fine. This makes sense because the focus last year was on phonics and literal comprehension. These new skills have more to do with figurative comprehension (understanding the bigger picture), and often take some time for students to grasp. Let's see if we can come up with some discussion activities that will encourage this new kind of thinking."
"The problem is you aren't challenging her. She is really gifted and she's just plain bored. That's why she doesn't complete her work."	*She is gifted—at wrapping her parents around her finger. Maybe she is a little lazy and shouldn't be allowed to get away with it!*	"Of course Annie is bright, and I agree that school should be challenging. Why don't we ask Mrs. Cobb, our gifted and talented resource teacher to put together a folder of activities for Annie to pursue when she completes her class work? In this way she'll experience the satisfaction of completing her work in a timely way and then can move on to material that she may find more challenging."
"You give too much homework. I'm not the only parent complaining. All the mothers are talking about it."	*She's stirring up trouble with all the parents.*	"Do you feel as though Brian is finding the homework difficult? As you know, our policy is ten minutes of homework per grade level. If it's taking longer than that we should find out if this has to do with his grasp of the material or something else. Let's set a date for a conference."

Conference/Call Log:
A Planning Template and Communication Record

At first, navigating through an uncomfortable exchange can feel awkward. By requesting a little time to think through the conversation ahead of time, you can choose some key phrases and "rehearse" the points you want to get across in a positive way.

When planning for a conversation, whether face to face or via the telephone, you might find the following planning template helpful. This one has been filled in, but a blank planning template follows on pages 67 and 68. Photocopy it to create a conference/call log. Not only will this help you plan your conversations with parents, but it will serve as a great record of each communication you have.

USING WORDS WISELY

There will be times when you'll be tempted to simply "tell it like it is" or to "say what you mean and mean what you say." In fact, we often hold up this kind of "honesty" as being assertive, courageous, and confident. But keep in mind the power of words—and the fact that a single incidence of "telling it like it is" (which often translates into "telling it as I see it") can permanently taint a relationship. In effect, you might wind up spending the balance of the school year paying for the satisfaction of "telling it like it is" on just one occasion! But, most important, choosing your words carefully ultimately creates an environment in which the best interest of the child is always protected.

Parent Conference Call Planner

Date of call/conference: _____

The issue clearly stated: _____

_____

The reason you're concerned (how this affects the child): _____

_____

_____

How I feel parents will respond: _____

_____

One positive anecdote to begin with: _____

_____

How I will phrase the problem in a positive, concerned manner: _____

_____

_____

_____

Describe the incident using specific examples in non-judgmental/objective language:

_____

_____

_____

Describe your concern about the effect this incident had on the student: _____

_____

_____

_____

What you hope to gain through the conversation: _____

_____

Recap the "action plan": _____

_____

After-contact follow-up notes: _____

_____

Whom you spoke to: _____

_____

Parent/guardian response: _____

_____

Next step: _____

_____

_____

_____

Chapter 6

Dealing With More Serious Issues

Cases of Neglect, Abuse, and Overbearing, Manipulative Parents

A little boy entered my class with a large band-aid peeking out of his shirt, in the small hollow where neck and shoulder meet. I smiled a little—it was such a peculiar place for a band-aid that I assumed he had a tiny boo-boo and had insisted, as youngsters often do, on an oversized bandage to heal a wounded spirit. I smiled at him and exclaimed, "Oh my, what a big band-aid! What happened to you?" He looked up at me for a moment with his enormous brown eyes, then looked down at his feet. He mumbled something. "I didn't hear you, sweetheart," I said. "Tell me again."

He sighed and shrugged a little. "My Daddy punched me," he mumbled.

I felt as though the wind had been knocked out of me. My heart started to pound. I didn't want to jump to any conclusions, tried to keep my voice calm.

"Were you . . . wrestling, you know, playing rough and he accidentally . . .?"

"No, my Daddy got mad and he punched me." He said it adamantly, the "p" sound in the word "punch" exploding angrily.

I felt sick inside. Suddenly so many little idiosyncrasies that this child had been displaying seemed to take on new and ominous meanings—the way he rarely made eye contact when spoken to, how another child could push some invisible button and instantly enrage him, how he often seemed to prefer his own company, indulging in fantasy games rather than joining in with others during free play.

I immediately reported the incident to my principal, who in turn called in the school nurse and social worker. By law, we had to report the incident to the State Department of Child Welfare Services, and we had to inform the parents. Of course, I wanted to do everything possible to protect this child. And though the thought of calling the parents to discuss this made me even more sick, it was a call that had to be made.

Through the years there have been other difficult situations—a call to a mother regarding her child's constant comments about her father's alcoholism; a conversation with a mother regarding her son's frequent public masturbation; a conference in which I had to share with his mother the extremely disturbing, possibly sociopathic drawings and writings of an eight-year-old boy; and a year-long relationship with an extremely overbearing, manipulative parent. Honestly, when I started off in the profession I never dreamed I'd be having these kinds of conversations and interactions with parents. In fact, the very thought of it would have been enough for me to consider a career-change before I ever set foot in a classroom. But, unfortunately, such incidents are a reality of the job, a job that is vitally important—possibly as important, even, as the difference between life and death.

In time, I learned when to script an awkward conversation beforehand (as I did in the examples mentioned above), when to seek counsel from support staff, and when to pass the situation on to others (an administrator, school psychologist, or social worker) who were specifically trained to deal with more challenging issues. The common thread in many of the scenarios I'll present in this chapter is abuse and/or neglect. Sometimes it's blatant, but other times it can be subtle. It is most often directed at the child, but it can also be directed toward the teacher. In either case, the recipient is made to feel defensive, ashamed, and taken advantage of.

> But, unfortunately, such incidents are a reality of the job, a job that is vitally important—possibly as important, even, as the difference between life and death.

Steps to Follow When You Suspect Child Abuse or Neglect

1. **First and foremost, talk to your administrator immediately.** Cases of abuse, neglect, or situations that place the child or others in danger, either physically or emotionally, cannot wait. It is critical for you to know the protocol for mandated reporting of abuse or neglect in your school. While laws for mandatory reporting remain consistent statewide, each school may have a slightly different protocol for making a report. Your principal needs to be informed, and support staff, such as the school psychologist, social worker or nurse, called in, according to your school or district protocol. These professionals can guide you through the process and lend support to the child, the family, and you.

   In most schools, the administration prefers to make this contact, thus leaving the teacher out of the immediate equation. This can be helpful in that any defensiveness or retaliatory verbal abuse will often bypass the teacher, allowing the teacher to maintain a more comfortable working relationship with parents and child. **Keep in mind, however, that regardless of what your administrator says, you have a legal obligation to notify authorities if you suspect abuse or neglect.** If you are uncertain about the laws in your particular state with regard to this, contact your state department of education, your state child welfare department, or your local, state, or national teachers' professional organization for guidelines.

On the Web

You may find the following Web sites helpful:

The National Exchange Club Foundation's Site: **www.preventchildabuse.com**

Prevent Child Abuse America: **www.preventchildabuse.org**

Child Welfare League of America: **www.cwla.org**

Stop Family Violence (advocacy): **www.stopfamilyviolence.org**

Stop it Now (sexual abuse prevention): **www.stopitnow.com**

2. **Document each conversation or questionable incident.** One year I watched a little boy come through my door each morning, the grime on his small hands thicker with each passing day, the narrow band of his underpants, perpetually inside out and unchanged, each day a little grayer than the day before, gaping out of the top of his filthy, baggy hand-me-down trousers. His hair hung in oily strands across his forehead. The school had already been in touch with Child Welfare Services, and it became my job to document his day-to-day demise. As heart wrenching as it was, my journal provided the necessary impetus for an eventual hygiene plan between the family and the school. (On his way into the building each morning he would discretely visit the school nurse, who would wash him up, launder his clothes, and shampoo his hair on a regular basis.) When documenting your concerns, be sure to use direct quotes of the child's words; this is much more valuable than paraphrasing, which can alter meaning based on your interpretation of what was said.

3. **Consult with support staff and the previous year's teacher.** No one wants to make an unfortunate, unfounded accusation. If you suspect any kind of abuse or neglect, a problem with alcohol or drug abuse, serious emotional or psychological problems, document the incidents in question, describe them in a narrative account (keep it objective—what you saw, what was said, and so forth), list the frequency with dates and times, consult with the child's previous teachers, the principal, the school psychologist, and the social worker. Many times previous teachers can "fill in the blanks" with respect to family history, behavioral issues, and any contact that was made with the family.

Here are some guiding questions to help you gather critical information:

◎ Have there been similar concerns in the past?
◎ Have these issues been addressed with the family before?
◎ Is there a pattern of behavior?
◎ If this has been ongoing, what was the family's reaction to the situation?
◎ Are there similar concerns with other siblings?
◎ Has there been intervention of any kind?

After speaking with a number of staff members individually, you might want to call a "Child Study" meeting—an informal meeting of staff and administration to discuss your observations, to review what's been done in the past, and to formulate an action plan. Check with your administrator to clarify school policy in such matters.

4. If you have to have a difficult conversation, "script" it first.
Communications of this nature should never be off the cuff. Sit down and write out what you plan to say. Choose your words carefully, keeping in mind that nothing will be gained by accusing or shocking a parent, and, in fact, the child could wind up bearing the brunt of the parent's frustration. Sit down and write out an objective account of what the child has demonstrated or said. Check your language for any unnecessary negative connotations. Also, by working through "what-ifs," play out all of the possible responses that a parent might present. What if the parent says this is none of your business? What if the parent says you've misinterpreted the situation? You must have a response ready for all of the possible "what-ifs," and be prepared to respond with a noncommittal "let me think about that and call you back" in cases where you might need time to process, research, or consult with staff.

A close friend of mine, Donna Miller, is the Executive Director of the Child Abuse Prevention Center in Stamford, Connecticut, and specializes in parenting issues. I asked Donna for some tips on maintaining communications with parents in the midst of cases involving abuse and/or neglect. Here is her list of suggestions:

◎ Whenever possible, have the school social worker or psychologist make the initial contact. In this way, the teacher can maintain a more natural relationship with the family and the student.

◎ If you find yourself having to make the initial contact with the parent, begin with an objective, non-judgmental report of what the child said or demonstrated: "Mrs. Dailey, I'm concerned because Katherine told me that her black eye was caused by being hit by her father." Whenever possible, this contact should be made in person, rather than over the telephone.

◎ Explain that the school is mandated to report the incident to the state child welfare agency. The parent might deny the incident or defend the action. Don't argue—it's not your role to interrogate; simply respond by saying, "I see. Well, as you may know, the school is required by law to report this incident to the Department of Child Services. What will happen is that a representative will contact you to sort through this."

◎ Make an attempt to validate the parent in some way and offer support. "I am aware of the tremendous pressure you've been under lately, and I know first-hand how challenging parenting can be. Keep in mind that the school is here to offer support and services to help the family work this through." Know specifically what kind of support or referral services your school is prepared to offer and share these with the parents.

Understanding the Dynamics of Ineffective Parenting

Offering validation is perhaps the hardest step in the process, as you may feel tremendous anger or even disgust with the parent. However, alienating the parent will only add fuel to the fire, and may serve to cut off the only avenue of communication with the family. The goal is to support and educate, not to humiliate or alienate. In fact, if the parent is humiliated, the child may pay the price.

"Parents who abuse or neglect are parents who are struggling," Donna Miller says. "They are parents who lack the skills needed to parent effectively. They also lack the coping skills necessary for dealing with everyday problems." She explains that this causes these parents to lash out at the weakest among them—the child. Later, they often feel deeply ashamed and overwhelmed.

Acknowledging the difficulty inherent in parenting, recognizing the stress in their present situation, and validating them in their efforts, however ineffective their efforts may be, can go a long way toward keeping the lines of communication open. It can also defuse defensiveness and encourage an openness to the idea of a rehabilitative program.

Donna also feels that it's important to understand the dynamics involved with parents who abuse or neglect a child. While this understanding does not justify an abusive act, it allows you to view the parent as someone who needs to be educated and supported rather than cut off and punished.

Donna describes the following four types of parenting styles:

FOUR STYLES OF PARENTING

1. **The Reactionary Parent:** This parent gives little or no forethought to parenting, basically allowing things to unfold on their own. The parent reacts in the moment to whatever the child might do. This style can work fine until the child does something that the parent dislikes. Then he or she often reacts inappropriately.

2. **The Corporal Punisher:** This parent believes that hitting, physically punishing, or even belittling the child is the correct thing to do. He or she often views the child as a possession, and as such, sees corporal punishment as a right and responsibility.

3. **The Permissive Parent:** The permissive parent views himself/herself as the child's friend, often giving over most of the decision-making to the child. When the child misbehaves, this parent feels embarrassed and betrayed, and out of these feelings, may lash out.

4. **The Positive Parent:** The positive parent educates the child by setting clear, consistent expectations for good behavior and fair consequences for misbehavior. The parent actually practices the behaviors expected of the child. The keys here are forethought, respect, and follow-through.

You can see how the first three parenting styles can lead to abusive situations. But, by maintaining open lines of communication with parents, the teacher can serve as a positive vehicle for gently moving ineffective, reactionary, permissive parents, or corporal punishers toward becoming positive parents, with the child being the chief beneficiary. Remember, your feelings about the parents are secondary to the best interest of the child. And nobody gains more through improved parenting than children.

Strategies for Dealing With the Overbearing, Manipulative Parent

A colleague of mine told me a story about an extremely critical, overbearing, and manipulative father whose presence over the course of the school year almost made this seasoned teacher leave the profession. This man constantly reminded the teacher that her salary was being paid by his tax dollars, that she was, after all, a public servant, and therefore beholden to the demands of the public, and that he had a good lawyer to defend his rights as a taxpayer if he were in any way dissatisfied with the education his son received. He would barge into the classroom during class time to "talk about a critical matter," was caught looking through papers on top of the teacher's desk while the class was in the cafeteria, and tried to bring a tape recorder to the parent-teacher conference in order to "document" the exchange.

While this is an extreme case, most of us have had to deal with a parent with at least some of these tendencies. It might be that a parent demands a daily written report on her child's progress, a request which you feel is excessive, overly time-consuming, and not in the best interest of the child. You might have a passive-aggressive parent who, despite numerous reminders about scheduled conference times, plants herself at your door each and every morning, always with a sweet smile and an apology, refusing to let go of your ear before the bell rings. Another parent might, despite school rules to the contrary, show up for her child's birthday with a magician, pizza, and a make-your-own sundae buffet. Or perhaps you have a parent who has gotten hold of your home phone number and calls you at all hours, weekends and holidays included. These are the parents to whom you'd most like to give a piece of your mind, to ask, "Are you for real, or what?" They do not respect boundaries, they ignore the rules, take advantage of your good nature, and treat you more like a public servant than a respected professional. These are all forms of subtle abuse, all demonstrating a blatant disregard for your professionalism.

What are some techniques for dealing with these stubborn, frustrating people and predicaments?

The Broken Record

After you've explained, for the third time, why you cannot have a conference today, and the parent continues to wheedle and cajole, and actually attempts to suck you into a conversation that you are determined not to have at that particular time, try the "Broken Record." The technique works something like this:

Parent:	Yes, but I really need to talk to you today.
Teacher:	As I mentioned, I have a PPT meeting in five minutes, so let's schedule . . .
Parent:	Sharon was upset again last night about her homework, don't you think . . .
Teacher:	As I mentioned, I have a PPT meeting (checking watch) in a few minutes. (Begins to gather up papers and briefcase. Shuts off the light.) I will call you this evening to schedule our conference when I can give you my full attention.
Parent:	It was the math again. It's always math that gives her trouble.
Teacher:	I have to leave for that meeting now, Mrs. Smith. I'll call you this evening. (Smiles, touches Mrs. Smith's arm, nods, and steps out of the door.)

The key to the "Broken Record" is to refuse to pick up the thread of the parents' conversation at that time, but to follow up as soon as possible at a reasonable time. Also, smile, nod, and continue to do what needs to be done. The technique is a little harder on the telephone. Over the phone, it's critical to maintain a pleasant, patient tone of voice, and to repeat the message: "As you know, I'm unable to take calls at home after 6:30. I'll be happy to meet with you tomorrow before school, at 7:45. Does that work?" If the parent continues, repeat, "Yes, but as you know, I'm unable to talk now. Does tomorrow morning work for you?"

Eventually, the parent will get the message.

The Sit-Back-and-Listen Technique

A parent storms into your room after school and begins to yell and berate you. You can't get a word in. Every time you try to speak, you're interrupted, and the verbal abuse escalates. In a situation like this, the best thing to do is to sit back and allow the parent to vent. Don't try to interrupt, correct the parent, or defend yourself. Let this person continue to vent until he or she runs out of steam.

It's important to understand that when someone is behaving in this way, they're primarily being driven by a need to release their displaced anger and frustration. They're NOT emotionally able to listen to reason or to problem solve until the anger has dissipated.

This kind of emotional outburst has a very limited life expectancy. By not immediately responding you accomplish several things:

- ◎ You make it clear, in a gentle way, that you will not respond to someone addressing you in a rude or derogatory manner.
- ◎ You model appropriate behavior for the other person.
- ◎ You do not run the risk of antagonizing the person further, thus escalating the verbal assault.
- ◎ You do not, inadvertently, find yourself drawn into an argument that you cannot win, and in which you might say something that you'll later regret.
- ◎ You maintain your dignity and professionalism.

After several minutes, when the parent has finished, take a deep breath and respond in a soft, calm voice. The objective is to allow the parent to know that you understand how upset he or she is, and that you really want to help. You can offer to meet at another time when you're both feeling calmer, or you can invite a mediator to join you. Here is how you might play this out:

"I'm so sorry to see you this upset. Please, let me get you a glass of water, or perhaps a cup of coffee." (If the parent agrees, this allows more time for a cooling down period. You can also use the opportunity outside the classroom to alert a colleague to make his or her presence known—another good means of encouraging appropriate behavior.) *"I'd really like to spend some time working this through with you. Is there an afternoon this week when we can set aside the necessary time to discuss this? Also, I'd be happy to invite our principal, Mrs. Stone, in to sort this out with us."*

If the yelling begins again, wait until it subsides before responding. *"I'm having a difficult time thinking this through clearly while you're this upset. I think it best that we get together at a time when we can discuss this calmly."*

If the parent persists, you must be quietly assertive. *"I really cannot be helpful to you under these circumstances and I have to insist that we discuss this calmly. If that cannot happen here today, we'll need to meet at another time."* (Here get up and begin moving toward the door.) If at any time you feel physically threatened, leave the room immediately and notify a colleague.

Prevention Is the Best Medicine

In talking to my colleagues over the years, I've concluded that there are a number of boundaries that overbearing or manipulative parents tend to cross. Have you had parents stretch or cross boundaries in any of the following ways:

- creating interruptions during class time?
- making intrusive telephone calls to you at home?
- showing a lack of respect for your privacy through inappropriate access to your desk and student records?
- disregarding classroom or school rules and policies?

When you suspect early on that a parent will not respect your rules, boundaries, and professionalism, take steps to prevent or head off these behaviors before a pattern becomes established and the situation gets out of hand.

For example, I had a parent volunteer who would often wander into my classroom when the class was at gym or the media center. She would look over student work (not only her child's, but other students' as well), glance at my plan book on my desk, and generally fail to respect my privacy or the privacy of the students in my class. I immediately began locking the door when we left the room, thus eliminating the opportunity for this kind of behavior.

If a parent consistently calls you at home after hours, screen your calls through your answering machine or caller I.D. Make it a policy never to take a call outside of those hours, no exceptions.

In response to the parent who barges in during class time, make a sign to display on the outside of your classroom door: LEARNING TAKING PLACE. PLEASE DO NOT DISTURB. FEEL FREE TO LEAVE A MESSAGE AT THE OFFICE.

Then, keep your door closed. If the parent comes in anyway, do not interrupt your teaching. Do not move toward the door or to the periphery of the classroom. In as pleasant a voice as you can muster say, "I'm sorry, but we can't be disturbed right now. Please leave me a note at the office." Then immediately go back to teaching and ignore the intrusive parent.

Other Sources: Help From Your Building Administrator and Your Local Education Association or Teacher's Union

Remember the overbearing, manipulative, threatening father who nearly drove the veteran teacher out of the profession? This was not a good relationship that went suddenly bad; the teacher sensed from the very first exchange that this would be a rocky relationship at best, and that there were issues for this parent that extended beyond the realm of the ordinary. It wasn't long before the teacher had tried—and exhausted—all of the usual "prevention" steps suggested above.

In cases like this you need to talk to your building administrator and keep a running record of your contacts with the parent. Perhaps the administrator will intervene, especially when the behavior begins to have a negative impact on your ability to teach. Many times this type of parent is deeply insecure and needs attention, affirmation, and support beyond what the classroom teacher can provide. The principal, either personally or through a referral to qualified support staff, may be able to provide some of the attention this parent is seeking.

You can also contact your local education association or teacher's union. These professional organizations can prove to be excellent resources in difficult cases. They'll inform you of your legal rights as well as your professional contractual commitments and responsibilities. These organizations offer not only practical advice, but legal counsel for their members. Just knowing that you have this kind of professional support takes a lot of the intimidation out of a situation in which a parent bullies you in any way.

Additionally, your local, state, and national professional organizations frequently offer workshops and training on a wide array of legal and professional issues that might turn up. It is always worthwhile to take advantage of these types of programs.

Conclusion

If you lay the proper foundation, most communications with parents will result in positive professional relationships, ones that often continue far beyond the year that the child was in your class. All of the hard work that you did to nurture these relationships will be paid back through the growth you see in your students, and in the gratitude expressed to you through the families you've touched. Your efforts will certainly make your job easier— but more important, they will positively affect the well-being and social/emotional growth of the children you teach.

Remember, even in the best relationships there are bound to be uncomfortable moments and misunderstandings. Knowing in advance how to deal with these issues can eliminate damaging, reactive behaviors that leave you feeling less than professional and can also help prevent the burn-out that comes from the repressed frustration of feeling as though others are walking all over you.

In fact, having the tools to navigate successfully through the entire spectrum of parent-teacher communications will not only make you feel capable and in charge, but will allow you the freedom to place most of your energy where it needs to be— in the teaching of children!